Our work at the University of Redlands is to serve students but the purposes of that work are much greater. In a very real sense we exist to serve our society and our world by preserving and transmitting the values of the liberal arts. That is the cause for which we are joined and the one that, together, we must continue to advance.

UNIVERSITY of REDLANDS

MEMORIES OF THEE WE LOVE SO WELL

Photographed by

ROBERT HOLMES

Harmony House

Publishers Louisville

We would like to thank the following people for their help in bringing this book from idea to reality: The 1990-91 Alumni Association Board of Directors, especially Bill Hardy '66 and Bill Dickenson '64; the staffs of Armacost Library, University Relations, and Alumni Relations, particularly Fred Hearth, Scot Allen '82 and Sharilyn Bailey '87; Registrar Emerita Esther Mertins for her work on the chronology; Julie Wieschendorff '91; Edith R. White Distinguished Professor of English and Literature Bruce McAllister; and our 1991-92 Alumni Association President, Mike McDowell '74. Most central to the success of this project were the efforts of Gretchen Peterson Lohnes '48, whose archival research uncovered the wonderful photographs in the heritage section; and to Larry E. Burgess '67, for his most engaging short history, his witty captions, and his unfailing good advice. *MHB*

Executive Editors: William Butler and William Strode
Library of Congress Catalog Number: 91-75132
Hardcover International Standard Book Number 0-916509-99-0
Printed in The Republic of Korea by Sung In Printing Company, LTD.
through Vivid Color Separation, New York, N.Y.
First Edition printed Spring, 1992 by Harmony House Publishers,
P.O. Box 90, Prospect, Kentucky 40059 (502) 228-2010 / 228-4446

Additional photography by Scott Allen '82 and Carol Appleton

INTRODUCTION

By James R. Appleton
Eighth President of the University of Redlands

In the life of an institution conceived before radio or silent movies, my few years here have been but the blink of an eye. Yet as I look across this campus I can see easily in its magnificent oaks, tranquil walkways and stately buildings the eras so many of you have evoked for me. As a university colleague and good friend said recently, "The past *and* the future are here in the present, if we'll only look." This book, *Memories of Thee We Love So Well*, is a portrait of the University of Redlands, yours and mine — its faces past and present, and the future promises those faces carry.

O, that dear old U of R,
Thy children near and far
Will sing to thee and all thy glories tell;
Where the orange blossoms grow
And the waters gently flow,
That dear old U of R we love so well.

Born of the passionate interests of a southern California citrus town in having its own private university and built on the humble site of an old winery and brickyard, the University of Redlands has become, in national rankings today, one of the finest colleges and universities in the Western United States, and one of a handful of universities in the country fully committed to liberal arts values while also offering select professional and graduate degrees. Although the final measure that society may apply to a university is its ability to inculcate employable skills in its students, rather than the wisdom they might need to get along with neighbors or self, we at the University of Redlands educate for *life* in at least the same proportion that we educate for *livelihood*. We have always balanced knowledge and values, education and the real world . . . or, in the words of founder Jasper Newton Field, the *mind* and the *heart*.

O, that dear old U of R,
Whose emblem shines afar,
Eternal as the hills we love so well;
Where the mountains tall and grand
Like an inspiration stand
That dear old U of R we love so well.

A teaching and learning community, writes educator Parker J. Palmer, must offer two kinds of love. "The first," he writes, "is the *love of learning itself.* The simple ability to take sheer joy in having a new idea, reaffirming or discarding an old one, connecting two or more notions that had hitherto seemed alien to each other, sheer joy in building images of reality with words, or music, or palettes that now suddenly seem more like mirrors of truth — this is the love of learning. And the second kind of love is *love of learners*, of those we see every day — who wax hot and cold, who sometimes want truth and sometimes evade it at all costs, but who are in our care and who, for their own sake, ours, and the world's, deserve all the love that the community of teaching and learning has to offer." These two loves will always be characteristic of Redlands, as those who have been touched by both know.

O, that dear old U of R,
The years can never mar
The memories of thee we love so well;
Where the friendships are so dear
That we leave them with a tear,
That dear old U of R we love so well.

There is tangible excitement in the air these days at the University of Redlands, the kind a community feels at the beginning of a journey that promises exhilaration, discovery and achievement. In 1911 Jasper Newton Field exhorted the University family not to rest on its laurels, but to "look up and toil on until we have achieved greater things than we have yet known." The year before he had spoken on that same community's behalf, resolving "that with God helping us we would establish not a third-rate nor second-rate, but a first-rate institution or none at all." The University of Redlands has never been content with mediocrity or a resting on laurels, and it has always been determined to learn from life's lessons. While we may see the many wonderful possibilities for this University's future, we also know the work that any bright future demands of us . . . on our journey toward it.

M
E
L
R
O
S
E
U OF 1923 R

REDLANDS THROUGH THE YEARS

The story of the University of Redlands at 85 years is the story of an institution much changed from its founding, yet one unchanged in spirit from its original commitment to educate not only the mind but also the heart. A peculiar set of circumstances led to the birth of a University of Redlands, California: the devastating 1906 San Francisco earthquake that destroyed the hopes for success with educational plans there; the failure of an American Baptist college in Los Angeles; the determination of businessmen in Redlands; and the energetic skill of the Rev. Jasper Newton Field. Dr. Field sought "this prize" for his city, urging first his parishioners at the First Baptist Church and then the Redlands Board of Trade to convince the American Baptist committee to locate its new university in Redlands.

Weeks of intense work, lobbying and personal visits, a persuasive gift of land from Karl C. Wells, and more than $50,000 from a city subscription drive captured the site committee's attention. Chartered on November 25, 1907, the University admitted its first students in September, 1909. The intervening year was used to hone concepts, hire faculty, determine academic policy, and plan the campus.

When surveying the present campus, it is difficult to imagine the humble beginnings of the University. Indeed, an old winery and the decadent remains of a brickyard marked the place where the University campus was to be. It was a discouraging scene to the nine professors and 52 students who arrived to form the first University community. Still, a hardy first graduating class of four proudly accepted their dipolmas in June, 1910.

By 1913, Woodrow Wilson had replaced William Taft as U.S. President, income tax had become law, and an energetic band of undergraduates had begun construction of the huge "R" in the local mountains. Also that year, the City of Redlands — its entire economy bound up in its world-famous navel oranges — experienced a devastating freeze which destroyed the crops and many trees. The University suffered greatly. But offers of extended credit, continued faith among those who supported the school and some deferred billing saw the young school through the crisis.

By the time World War I began, the construction of Bekins Hall and the President's Mansion (now the Alumni House) had begun to give form to the campus. Most significant during these years was the commitment to the liberal arts tradition, and to the education of students who would be sent forth to do good and undertake service to improve the world. However, with Field's resignation in 1915 and the problems of the Great War and the recession of 1919-20, the University growth again was restrained.

Guiding the University during the decade of the 1920s was Victor Leroy Duke, a member of the original faculty and a man of vision. Duke and the trustees rejoiced in a Rockefeller Foundation grant which enabled great strides to be made academically. New dormitories were added to the residential campus, additional classrooms were built, a handsome Memorial Chapel anchored the north end of the quad, and the Alma Mater as we now know it was unequivocably adopted. The University was taking its place as a fine private undergraduate institution.

The Depression brought change. (Herbert Hoover was out, Franklin Roosevelt was in.) President Duke died suddenly, leaving a campus in mourning but a campus intact and vigorous. The 1930s brought campus rapport and an influx of educated, bright and challenging faculty. Clarence Howe Thurber became the third president and upgraded the academic curriculum. Thurber resigned in 1936 and the University struggled within itself for a sense of direction.

When he said to the selection committee, "Do you think I am the man for the job?", it was clear that in Elam J. Anderson the University would have a new president of singular determination and will. Anderson minced no words. He was aware of the religious beginnings of the University, and he was also committed to its academic excellence. He was not afraid of trustees and he defended many of his faculty in a sensitive transition from "regional" university to "university with national outlook." No one knew that the 1940s would bring even more calamity into a world already besieged with problems. World War II profoundly changed the University. With Elam Anderson's sudden death in 1944 and with V-12 units taking classes at Redlands, the school was in for a new phase in its growth.

With the building of a new Commons and the arrival of a new president from the East — George H. Armacost — a new period of University life began in 1945. It was a time of continuity, new social life developments, vigorous building campaigns, and increased endowment. The post-war years saw veterans as students, and the dorms nearly burst their seams.

During the 1950s, the University had reached maturity based on its commitment 50 years earlier. Enhanced and encouraged by its proven capacity to change and grow, Redlands responded to the needs of its students with academic innovations, construction of more dormitories and enlargement of other facilities. Academic and athletic achievements reached a new high and innovations in student living were effected at a swift pace.

As the 1960s evolved, it was as if one era had come to a close and another taken its place almost at once — a new era which ushered in a national atmosphere charged with acrimony, debate and confrontation. Vietnam was upon us. The University experienced little of the travail which convulsed some other institutions of higher learning, but changes came nonetheless. As George Armacost retired in 1970 after 25 years of service, baby-boom students were no more, inflation began and then recession, and an experimental cluster college known as Johnston was begun at the University.

The presidency of Eugene E. Dawson came about as a nation examined and agonized over its foreign policy and domestic instincts and experienced what economists said could never happen: unemployment, inflation, and an economic uncertainty called "stagflation."

Meanwhile, curricular changes, vocational shifts and a declining student pool began to affect American colleges. The University of Redlands was not invulnerable to this trend and thus turned its attention from adding to its capital facilities to the imperatives of increasing its endowment, providing more student scholarships, and realistically dealing with tuition costs.

Certain curricular emphases from the 1960s provided positive experiences and patterns for Redlands in the 1970s; excellence in scientific programs, foreign study opportunities, and a still firm commitment to the liberal arts. The University recognized the additional need to provide educational opportunities for working adults with the establishment of the Alfred North Whitehead Center for Lifelong Learning (at first a cluster college). Whitehead was designed to offer undergraduate and graduate programs for the mature student by responding to contemporary trends in higher education and the needs of the workplace.

The end of the 1970s brought about intense discussions and a firm resolve to secure the University's future and keep undiminished its purpose of liberal arts education with quality. Following the resignation of Dr. Dawson in 1978, President Douglas R. Moore inherited an institution facing the challenges imposed on all of private higher education: less money, higher costs, fewer students. Under Moore's leadership the concept of "partnership" between the various elements of the University became the human priority. The operational priority became the commitment to a capital campaign to enlarge the endowment dramatically. In order to accomplish this important new thrust in direction, new alignments in the structure of Whitehead and Johnston Center, an academic prioritization, the raising of the academic standards at entrance for students, and the re-shaping of the Board of Trustees became major challenges and accomplishments during this period.

By 1987, the first capital campaign in Redlands history became a real plan. The themes were chosen and much of the detailed work completed. Then Doug Moore suffered a heart attack, underwent major surgery and convalescence, and died suddenly in March.

A saddened campus put many of its decisions on hold. A trustee selection committee, still numb from the tragedy, pushed forward with a search for a new president. By September, 1987, the selection committee focused upon one candidate. After intense interviews in which the campus scrutinized the candidate and the candidate scrutinized the University, a unanimous consensus was achieved and James R. Appleton, vice president for development at the University of Southern California, accepted the appointment.

Dr. Appleton, with wide experience and an excellent background involving both university administration and an understanding of students, (as a dean of student life), brought to the campus an energy and determination to carry out past plans, but equally important, to create and innovate his own agenda. He joined the University community in November, 1987.

This is what the University is all about: not content to suffer mediocrity, willing to learn from its travails, the University of Redlands has always remained part of the world, committed to sending out graduates who seek to improve the world. The possibilities for the University, for its staff, faculty, students, alumni and friends are illimitable. The original resolve remains bright: "to serve the mind and the heart."

—Larry E. Burgess '67, Ph.D.

The Awakening
The Awakening

It is our solemn duty as educators to send forth leaders with knowledge and understanding but also with the concept of a divine purpose . . . . The challenge to education in the century ahead is much greater, for the aim is not material success but character development. Education must be dominated by the ideals of fellowship, brotherly love, service, and the understanding of human aspirations and motives.

President George H. Armacost, from his inauguration address

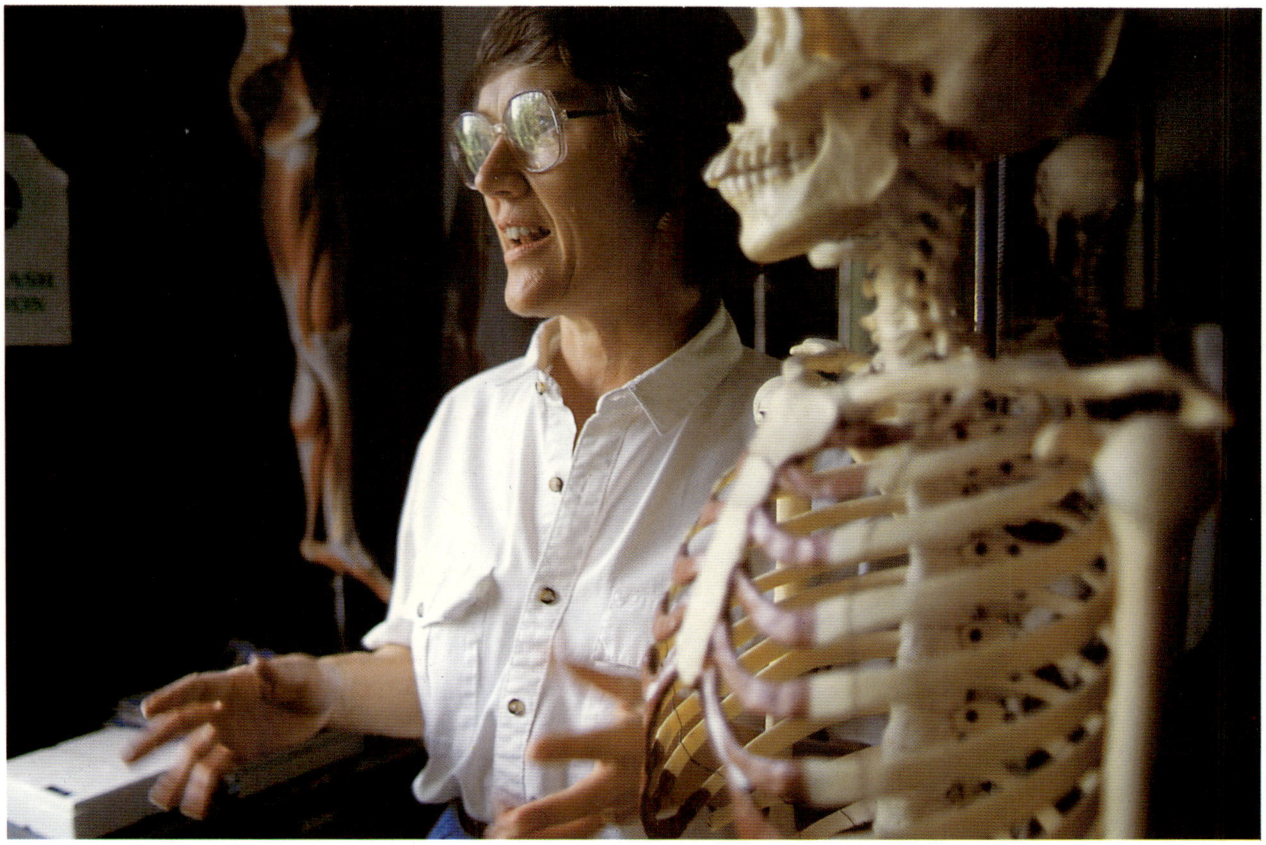

LARSEN HA

The business of campus life is part of the view from my window. I see students, relaxing or playing frisbee in the warm afternoon sunlight, others crossing on their way to class or to the library, the playing fields, or to visit friends. Nearly their whole lives lie ahead of them; they face the magic and mystery of their futures.

President Douglas R. Moore, *Redlands Magazine,* Spring 1986

Melrose Hall

JOHN W WILLIAMS
CONFERENCE CENTER

The great benefit of college is not that it builds your character, much less that it helps you make money or find a mate. The great benefit is that it stretches and enlarges your mind and helps you see the larger world beyond yourself more clearly and more fully.

James Q. Wilson '52

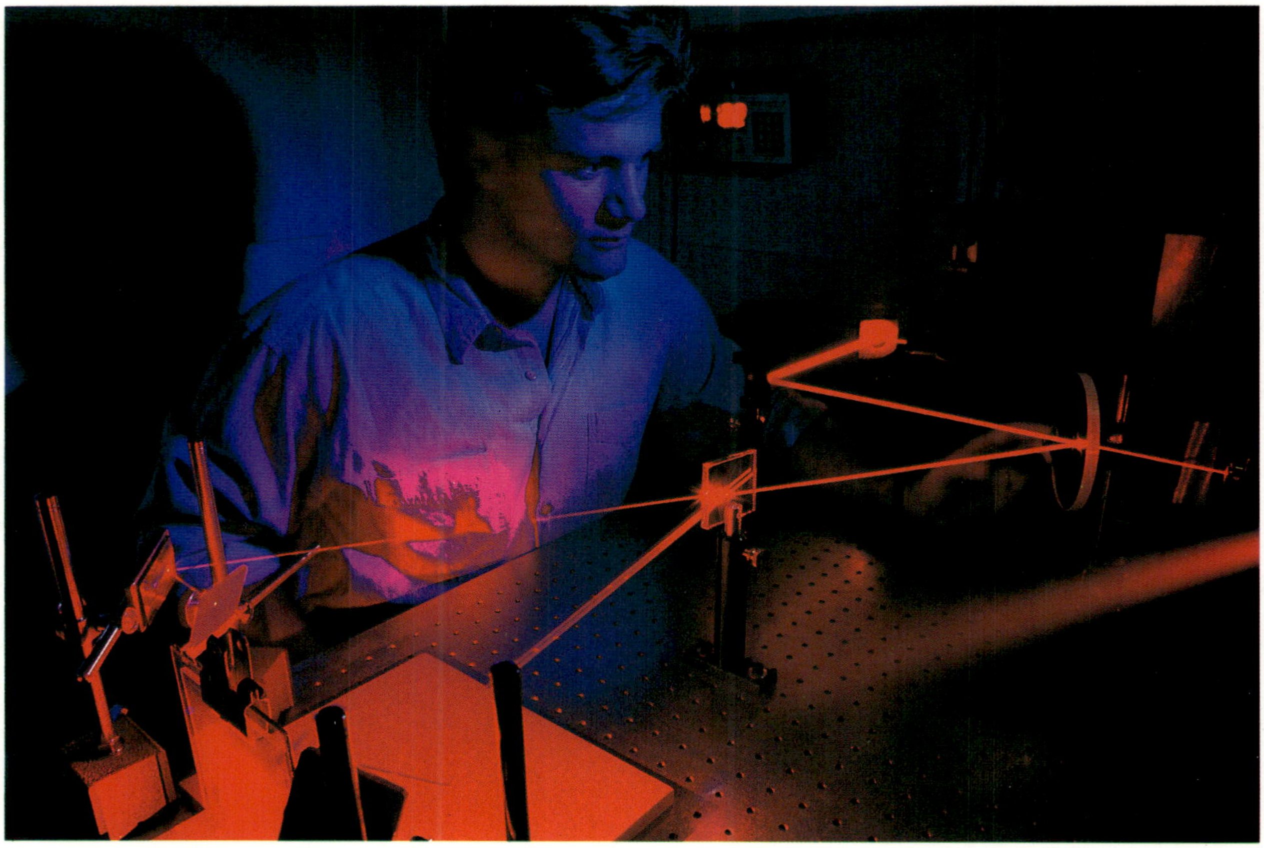

Jamie
Jamie

NATURAL ORANGE PACKERS
PURE GOLD
REDLANDS

ΑΘΦ

45
50
55
60
65
70
75

I work my head off to win every game, but I only hope that every kid who plays football for me comes out a better man.

Frank Serrao, from an article in *The Sun*, September 1972

46
60

Rubyfruit Jungle

V. 10am
came by.
Donna
Van-Trees
are in my
apartment
Donna
I am
in

Fairmont Hall

Och Tamale
Gazolly Gazump
Deyump Deyatty Yahoo,
Ink Damink
Deyatty Gazink
Deeyump Deray Yahoo,
Wing Wang
Tricky Trackey
Poo Foo
Joozy Woozy
Skizzle Wazzle
Wang Tang,
Orky Porky Dominorky

Alumni House

THE ZANJ
SUSAN JAMES
Merlyn Bonney
Dawn Romo

1931
HCC
HALF CENTURY
HALF CENTURY +
PLUS

UNIVERSITY
OF
REDLANDS

BA
'91

UNIVERSITY OF REDLANDS
REDLANDS

BA

The University of Redlands has had a long history of service. We have always taken pride in the fact that our students do care. There has always been a pervasive attitude at Redlands that individuals can have an impact on society, and our graduates feel an obligation to continue this tradition of involvement and contribution. This is reflected in the fact that more than one third of our graduates are in the field of education.

C. Stephen Hankins, Dean of Admissions, 1984

THANKS
MOM
+
DAD
University of Redlands
The Board of Trustees of the University
on recommendation of the Faculty and
by virtue of the authority granted by
law hereby confers upon
Ko Tamura
the degree of
Bachelor of Arts
with all the Rights, Privileges and Honors pertaining thereto
MAHALO
MOM

University of Redlands

R

MEMORIES...

The President's home on the later Hall of Letters site by the Administration Building. The foreground is now the tennis courts and Centennial Grove.

A look back at Redlands in photographs from the University archives

A SELECTED CHRONOLOGY OF REDLANDS

1907 University of Redlands incorporated. Mattison B. Jones elected President of Board of Trustees.

1909 Jasper Newton Field elected first president; Ground broken for Administration Building; Cornerstone laid for Administration Building; First meeting and organization of nine faculty members at the First Baptist Church; University of Redlands classes officially opened at the First Baptist Church in the College of Liberal Arts, College of Fine Arts and the Academy. Fifty-nine students enroll during the first year; Maroon and Grey adopted as school colors; Pi Chi (first social fraternity) founded.

1910 University classes moved to the Administration Building; Administration Building dedicated. Ground broken for Bekins Hall; Lumber from old winery used to build a gymnasium; Delta Kappa Psi (first social sorority) founded; First Zanja Fest (later Fiesta); First Commencement, with four bachelor of arts degrees conferred; *Spectrum* (first student publication) published; Bekins Hall for women opened; Ground broken for President's Mansion; College branch of Y.M.C.A. organized.

1911 College branch of Y.W.C.A. organized; The Athletic Association formed; Alpha Theta Phi Sorority founded; Pajamarino originated; Student body constitution adopted.

1912 Alumni Association organized.

1913 "The great freeze" threatens the economic life of the University; The "R" is created on a local mountain; Ashel Cunningham named as athletic coach; First freshman class cleans the "R."

1914 Alpha Sigma Pi Sorority organized; President Field retires; Phi Kappa Delta, forensic honor society formed; President's Mansion becomes Fine Arts Building used for College of Fine Arts until 1921; *Spectrum* (the student publication) becomes *The Campus*.

1915 George P. Cortner becomes business manager; First edition of *La Letra* named for the "R."

1916 President Victor Leroy Duke inaugurated as second president; Kappa Sigma Sigma Fraternity founded; Gymnasium destroyed by fire.

1918 Term "Bulldog" first used for athletic teams.

1918-19 Student Army Training Corps on campus.

1920 Cornerstone laid for Hall of Science (later Duke Hall); International Club organized by Prof. A. Collins.

1921 Beta Lambda Mu Sorority founded (went inactive in 1960, reactivated as Beta Lambda in 1989); New buildings include Fine Arts East, Fairmont dormitory for women, and California Hall for men; "Och Tamale" composed by C. Merle Waterman; President's Mansion renamed "Knoll Hall" becomes women's dormitory until 1925.

1922 Delta Alpha Honor (scholarship) Society organized by Professors H.C. Merrill, J.W. Kyle, and H.E. Marsh.

1923 Fine Arts West built; Alpha Gamma Nu Fraternity founded.

1924 Melrose Hall, dormitory for men, completed; School of Education formed; Approval by State Board of Education to issue teaching credentials; First issue of *U.R. Alumnus*.

1925 Grossmont Hall, dormitory for women, completed; President Duke took up residence in President's Mansion.

1926 Library dedicated (later Larsen Hall); Accreditation by Association of American Universities; Kappa Pi Zeta Sorority founded (went inactive in 1947).

1927 Alumni Greek Theatre completed; Infirmary built.

1928 Chapel dedicated; Casavant Organ dedicated by Pietro A. Yon, Vatican organist; Currier Gymnasium built; First annual Whiskerino originated by Milton Gair.

1929 New music hall (combination of Fine Arts East and West) completed; President's Mansion — in two parts — moved to Taylor Hill to make room for Hall of Letters.

1930 Hall of Letters dedicated.

1932 Hawaii Exchange Program established; First Writers' Week.

1933 President Duke dies of heart attack, Redlands SPURS founded; President James Thurber inaugurated.

1935 First mid-year commencement.

1936 Chi Sigma Chi Fraternity founded.

1937 Name of college newspaper changed from *The Campus* to *The Bulldog*.

1938 Dr. Elam J. Anderson becomes fourth president; First year of Yeomen sophomore service organization.

1939 University Hall (Casa Loma Hotel) purchased as a dormitory for men, became a dormitory for women in 1943; Religious Emphasis Week inaugurated.

1940 Alpha Chi Delta Sorority organized (went inactive in 1951).

1941 University Commons built; Mattison B. Jones, President of Board of Trustees, dies and was succeeded by Joy G. Jameson.

1943 Navy V-12 program begins on campus.

1945 Navy V-12 program ends; Dr. George H. Armacost inaugurated as fifth president of the University; Fifty units of government housing provided on campus for veterans.

1947 Sigma Kappa Alpha Fraternity founded (went inactive in 1952, reactivated in 1986); Chapel from Santa Ana air base provided by government to become the Little Theatre on campus until 1969; Fellows of the University founded; Feast of Lights program begins.

1948 Position of Executive Director for Alumni Association was created.

1949 Cortner Hall for men dedicated.

1951 Pi Chi and Kappa Sigma Sigma houses built on fraternity row.

1952 Student Union building, known as the "Dog House" completed; Watchorn Hall, gift of Mr. & Mrs. Robert Watchorn, built.

1954 Washington Semester program begins in cooperation with the American University of Washington, D.C.

1955 KUOR radio station established; Anderson Hall for women, named for Morton Anderson, constructed.

1956 Founders Hall for men built; Science Hall renamed Duke Hall in recognition of President Duke; Mortar Board honor society installed.

1957 Hornby Hall of Science built.

1958 North Hall for men built; Fiftieth anniversary celebration begins.

1960 Semester in Europe (Salzburg program) initiated.

1961 Casa Loma Room added to the Commons.

1963 Peppers Art Center (a gift from Tom and Ann Peppers); The Student Union, and Merriam Hall for men constructed.

1964 Hentschke Hall (a gift from the five Hentschke sisters) was built for engineering science.

1965 Bekins-Holt Hall for women built.

1966 Truesdail Speech Center opened.

1967 Glenn Wallichs Festival Theatre completed; 14-4-14 week academic calendar adopted.

1968 Stadium moved and new athletic facilities installed.

1969 New library constructed (later named the Armacost Library); "Coeducational" dormitories approved; Johnston College living learning center and two dormitories added to campus; Required chapel attendance discontinued; Johnston College opened with 181 students.

1970 President George Armacost retires; Eugene E. Dawson begins his term as the sixth president of the University.

1973 A new structure of six academic divisions established, each to be headed by a dean; Dr. Gordon Atkins named Dean of Special Programs; this division later became the Alfred North Whitehead College.

1974 The Jameson Center for the Study of Religion and Ethics begins.

1976 University reorganized into three colleges to be governed by one Board of Trustees: 1. The University of Redlands, Liberal Arts; 2. Johnston College, experimental and non-curricular; 3. Alfred North Whitehead College, for non-traditional students; Inaugural ceremonies for Whitehead College.

1977 Chapter of Phi Beta Kappa was installed; Proudian Interdisciplinary Honors Program activated; President Eugene Dawson retires.

1978 Inauguration of President Douglas R. Moore.

1979 University again reorganized with both Johnston College and Alfred North Whitehead College becoming programmatic divisions within the University.

1980-81 Johnston Center moves to new quarters in Bekins Hall; Alumni Relations Office moves to Alumni House (former President's Mansion); Whitehead Center moves to Williams Conference Center.

1982-83 Seventy-fifth anniversary year celebrations; Renovation of Orange Mill (in Willis Center) completed; Town & Gown founded.

1984 Maroon & Grey student service organization founded.

1987 Death of Dr. Douglas R. Moore.

1988 Inauguration of James R. Appleton as eighth president of the University.

1989 Phi Sigma Tau Fraternity founded.

1990 Trustees plan to raise $45 million in new endowment, capital enrichment and annual giving by 1993.

Austere and dignified, Dr. Jasper Newton Field could be a spellbinding orator. He lit the fires of service in Town and Gown and won a college for Redlands in 1907.

The first dorm, Bekins Hall, as it appeared to the eye in 1910. Note the lavish landscaping.

Dr. Field churns the earth for the 1908 ground breaking of the Administration Building site.

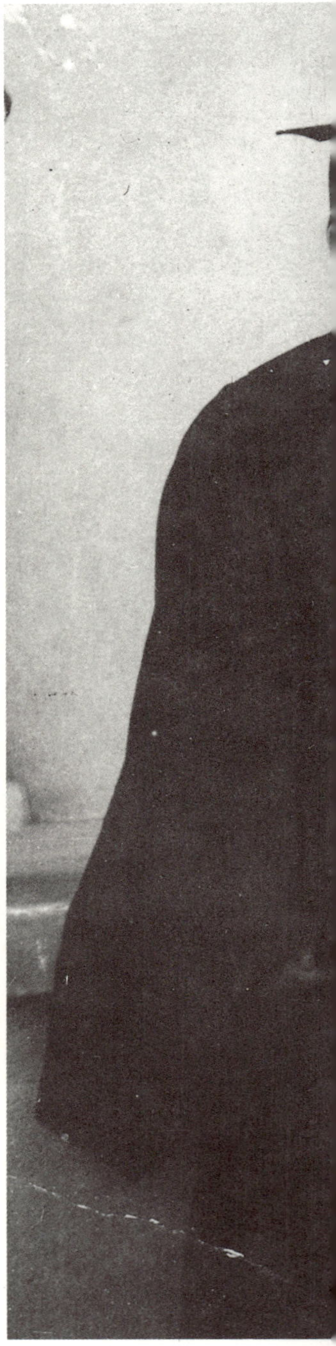

"A good example of religious toleration and in a denominational college. Seven graduates representing seven different religious denominations." Redlands Class of 1912, third graduating class.

Some of our most famous alumni came from this class of 1918. Here they are at the President's mansion, now the site of the Parker Hall of Letters.

George P. Cortner, whose tireless efforts kept Redlands going. He literally gave his life to the school.

Before zip codes, double digit stamps, and long lines, the postal service employed Dr. James W. Thorpe as the first mail carrier to the U of R in 1909. Thorpe, later a dentist in Redlands, was a young man in search of a job.

D.J. Stewart, bookstore manager of the "Dog House," is not handling buckets of beer.

The whole chapel would shake to its reinforced concrete rafters when Spelman unleashed the beautifully awesome Casavant organ.

A man of principle, President Victor Leroy Duke often intimidated adversaries but enjoyed much respect and esteem by Town and Gown.

Not a student protest — nor is this a holding tank. In pre-insurance hassle days, there was the charming event known as the "Frosh Brawl."

Sandy Scholton '67 no longer wears the frosh beanie as a school principal. And Bob Bishop '64, University Trustee, now eagerly speaks to freshmen.

Not a "sit in" during the '60s but an equally festive session: the annual Alpha Gamma Nu Noel.

With hands better placed for a golf putter, the symbolic shovel returns the earth which nurtured the university's birth.

The unwilling and unhappy at compulsory chapel. Now they say it was great and yearn for its return: we call them alumni.

These are not peeping Toms but students with V-12 unit sailors instructing these civilians on air patrol techniques during World War II.

A subversive gathering of sorority women. Note the hats: a clear sign of a plot to blur the image.

The oldest constantly-used water ditch in California—"The Zanja," pronounced "Sankee" by the locals. It runs through our campus.

Baseball in 1911 was barely able to compete with rugby. By World War I people would ask "What's rugby?".

Track and field has a distinguished history, including Olympic quality competition. Here are four of Southern California's most famous runners of the time: Lloyd Yount '23, Everest Zediker '23, William Yount '19, Colon Kilby '21.

Esther Williams, where are you?

Singer, stage and screen star, and father of Bonnie, John Raitt the shot putter with his coaching mentor, Cecil Alonzo Cushman.

Professor S. Guy Jones had every right to kick this ball. He would help out Walter Hentschke (holding) in the old days when the student teams were "one" short.

Imagine a tea with real tea, silver service, and canapes — at Homecoming. Note the social gaffe being committed by not balancing the tea cup.

Still an occasional tradition, the bonfire is rarely used to roast marshmallows.

Start 'em young and keep 'em going. Rah, rah, Redlands!
The little girl is Mary Armacost Hulst, now a trustee.

Sporting attire and racket size have changed but vigorous instruction continues. Was this posed?

The one constant in all U of R history — the food line — and the food!

The Gamma Nu Noel brought out the rugged and sartorial elegance of President Armacost.

Also a victim of liability insurance and lawyer paranoia was the beloved and fun-filled frolic, the Pajamarino. Of course, many students no longer wear pajamas.

Danny King '63 throws a pot. He and dozens of other students learned at the hand of the master, Professor Moburg.

Seeing only darkness, the student says "Okay, touch the two wires together and see what happens."

The Spurs — the service remains the same, but the dress is completely different.

"You'd better get the first question right, or your parents will cut your allowance," warns the GE College Bowl producer to senior Jackson Parham '66. From left to right, John Yeomans '66, Parham, Joe Lynn '67, Peter Gregora '67.

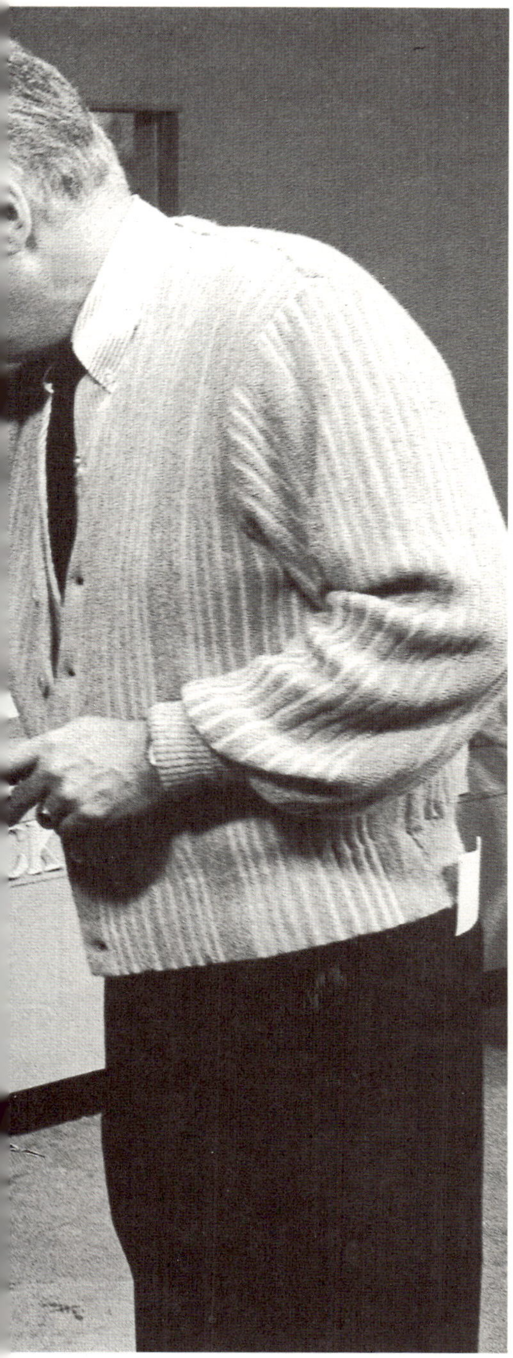

Bill Main, beloved professor, listens carefully to a question on General Electric's 1966 College Bowl. Redlands came close but lost to Wake Forest.

Today we call it aerobics. The challenge of dance tests skill and muscle; just try this if you doubt it.

Music has been an important part of Redlands since the School of Music was founded in 1909.

A chapel service featuring J. William Jones and the University Choir, with Margaret Dow at the organ. Who's counting the chapel slips?

Pre-computer days — they still managed to graduate the students looking on in 1965. Marc Jack Smith, President Armacost, Esther Mertins.

The National Championship debate team of 1952, Jim Wilson and Holt Spicer. In 1991 at Homecoming they defeated the 1991 National Championship U of R team.

A rehearsal for Zanja Fiesta at the Alumni Greek Theatre. The scripts were always a local effort by students and faculty.

The freeway to Redlands in the 1960s: Note a gentler time on the roads.

A staged kiss at the busy intersection of Colton and Orange Streets, the old Casa Loma Hotel, then University Hall.

TRIBUTE

This book is our way of thanking you, the alumni of the University of Redlands. As our eternal trustees, you have established and maintained the reputation of this University by what you achieved as students, and by the lives you have led since graduation — your professional accomplishments, your civic involvements and your tireless contribution of time, energy, and financial support to Redlands.

If you look closely, you will find yourselves in the pages of this book; not by face or name perhaps, but by the loyalty and love that assures the University of Redlands is alive and strong on the eighty-fifth anniversary of its founding.

Merilyn Bonney
Director, Alumni Relations
The University of Redlands

Schriften
der Wissenschaftlichen Gesellschaft in Straßburg
29. Heft

Die
Ebenbürtigkeitsfrage im Hause Croy

Von

Hermann Rehm

Straßburg
Karl J. Trübner
1916

Die

Ebenbürtigkeitsfrage im Hause Croy

Von

Hermann Rehm

Straßburg
Karl J. Trübner
1916

Druck von M. DuMont Schauberg, Straßburg.

Die Ebenbürtigkeitsfrage im Hause Croy.

Von

Hermann Rehm.

I. Das herzogliche Haus Croy hat die Stellung einer standesherrlichen Familie in Deutschland und daher das Recht der Ebenbürtigkeit, d. h. den Anspruch gegen die regierenden Familien, daß diese anerkennen, die Mitglieder des Hauses Croy besitzen den gleichen Geburtsstand wie Angehörige souveräner Geschlechter.

A. Nach dem Wortlaut des Art. 14 der deutschen Bundesakte vom 8. Juni 1815 ist das Geschlecht der Croy kein deutsch-hochadeliges, denn nach ihm wird die dort vorgesehene besondere Rechtsstellung eingeräumt nur Häusern, die seit 1806 mittelbar geworden und ehemals reichsständisch gewesen sind. Die Familie Croy ist seit 1806 mittelbar, d. h. anderer Staatsgewalt unterworfen geworden, aber sie ist nie reichsständisch gewesen. Allein dem Wortlaut der Bundesakte Art. 14 geht der Sinn dieser Bestimmung vor. Das BGB. § 133 stellt den Satz auf: „Bei der Auslegung einer Willenserklärung ist der wirkliche Wille zu erforschen und nicht an dem buchstäblichen Sinne des Ausdrucks zu haften." Die unmittelbare Geltungskraft dieser Bestimmung reicht nicht über das bürgerliche Recht hinaus, aber sie spricht für das bürgerliche Recht lediglich aus, was nach der Vernunft der Dinge für jeden Rechtsteil, daher auch für das öffentliche und deshalb auch für das Völkerrecht gilt. Die Auslegung hat in erster Linie nicht eine buchstäbliche, sondern eine logisch-historische zu sein. Rechtssätze sind nicht nach dem Wortlaut, sondern nach dem Sinne, nach dem Zusammenhang auszulegen. Aus dem Zusammenhang der deutschen Bundesakte mit der Wiener Kongreßakte vom 9. Juni 1815 folgt: der Herzog von Croy ist im Jahre 1806 mittelbar gewordener ehemaliger Reichsstand, zwar nicht nach dem Wortlaut, aber im Sinne von Art. 14 der deutschen Bundesakte. Der wirkliche Wille der in der Bundesakte eine Willenserklärung Abgebenden war, dem Herzog von Croy die bevorzugte Rechtsstellung eines seit 1806 mittelbar gewordenen ehemaligen Reichsstandes einzuräumen.

1. Gewiß konnten die Vertragschließenden von 1815 nicht einen neuen ehemaligen Reichsstand schaffen. Sie konnten mit Rechtswirkung nicht erklären: wir wollen, daß der Herzog von Croy Reichsstand „war". Ein solcher Rechtssatz wäre unverbindlich. Denn kein Mensch, also auch keine Regierung hat Macht über die Vergangenheit. Kein Menschen- und demgemäß auch kein Staatenwille kann Geschehenes ungeschehen und in der Vergangenheit Nichtgeschehenes in ihr geschehen machen. Die Staaten hatten lediglich die Macht zu erklären, wir glauben, der Herzog von Croy war Reichsstand, aber eine solche Erklärung ist keine Willens- sondern eine Meinungs-Erklärung, ein geschichtliches Urteil, eine Wissens-, aber keine Willens-Äußerung, kein Befehl und deshalb nicht verbindlich. Allein die deutschen Staaten haben 1815 weder das eine noch das andere erklärt, weder: wir wollen, noch: wir glauben, daß der Herzog Reichsstand war. Sondern ihre Erklärung lautet nur: wir wollen, daß der Herzog von Croy dieselbe bevorzugte Rechtsstellung besitze, die wir den seit 1806 mittelbar gewordenen ehemaligen Reichsständen einräumen; wir setzen den Herzog von Croy in dieselben Rechte ein, in die wir diese Reichsstände einsetzen. In dieser Bedeutung konnten die Staaten neue Reichsstände schaffen; sie konnten sie nicht geschichtlich, aber rechtlich erzeugen, sie konnten nicht ehemals reichsständische Häuser (s. Rehm, Prädikat- und Titelrecht der deutschen Standesherren 1905 S. 237), aber sie konnten neue deutsche Standesherrschaften (Rehm, a. a. O. S. 62) d. h. den Rechtssatz schaffen, daß Stände, die nicht Reichsstände waren, dieselben Vorrechte genießen sollen, wie sie den Ständen eingeräumt werden, die Reichsstände gewesen sind. Den Begriff Standesherr hat die Bundesakte erst geschaffen, nur der Begriff Reichsstand gehört der Vergangenheit an.

2. Daß der Herzog von Croy ein im Jahre 1806 mittelbar gewordener ehemaliger Reichsstand im Sinne von Art. 14 der Bundesakte, d. h. in dem Sinne ist, daß die Bundesakte ihn für die in Art. 14 eingeräumten Vorrechte den im Jahre 1806 mittelbar gewordenen ehemaligen Reichsständen gleichstellt, ergibt sich aus folgendem.

Die Wiener Kongreßakte nimmt an einigen Stellen auf die mittelbar gewordenen ehemaligen Reichsstände und insbesondere auf die Bundesakte Art. 14 Bezug. An einer Stelle tut sie es durch wörtliche Übersetzung. In Art. 58 Abs. 2 gibt sie die Vorschrift von Bundesakte Art. 6 Abs. 2: „Ob den mediatisierten vormaligen Reichsständen auch einige Kuriatstimmen in Pleno zugestanden werden sollen, wird die Bundesversammlung bei der Beratung der organischen Bundesgesetze in Erwägung nehmen" also wieder: La Diète, en s'occupant de lois organiques de la confédération, examinera, si on doit accorder quelques voix collectives aux anciens Etats de l'Empire médiatisés. Mediatisierte vormalige Reichsstände ist somit mit anciens Etats de l'Empire médiatisés übersetzt. In einem anderen Artikel — Art. 52 — ist mittelbar gewordene Reichsstände durch états médiatisés, also durch mediatisierte Stände wiedergegeben und zwar in besonderem Hinblick auf Art. 14 der Bundesakte, indem gesagt wird: „la principauté d'Isenbourg est placée sous la souveraineté de S. M. J. et R. A. (Autriche) et sera envers Elle dans les rapports que la constitution fédérative de l'Allemagne règlera pour les états médiatisés." In zwei weiteren Artikeln aber und zwar solchen, die vor den beiden bisher genannten stehen, ist das „mediatisierte ehemalige Reichsstände" nur mit territoires médiatisés wiedergegeben. Wir begegnen dem in Art. 32 und 43. An beiden Stellen geschieht es in unmittelbarer Beziehung zu Bundesakte Art. 14. Es wird gesprochen von den Verhältnissen, welche die deutsche Bundesakte für die mediatisierten Territorien regeln wird: les relations que la constitution fédérative de l' Allemagne règlera pour les territoires médiatisés (Art. 32 und 43). Wir sehen somit, nicht: „vormals reichsständische", sondern: „mittelbar gewordene" Territorien. Das Wesentliche erblickt die Kongreßakte daher nicht in der ehemaligen Reichsstandschaft, sondern in der vormaligen Landesherrlichkeit, Souveränität, Staatsgewalt.

3. Was für die Kongreßakte gilt, ist aber auch für die Bundesakte zu sagen. Die deutsche Bundesakte besteht aus zwei Teilen. Der erste, die Art. 1—11 umfassend, enthält die allgemeinen Bestimmungen und ist auch so überschrieben. Der zweite Abschnitt, die Art. 12—20 begreifend, trägt die Überschrift „Besondere Bestimmungen". Beide Teile sind in die Kongreßakte übernommen. Der Abschnitt „Allgemeine Bestimmungen" wörtlich: die Art. 1—11 der deutschen Bundesakte stehen in der Kongreßakte in französischer Sprache als Artikel 53 mit 63. Darauf folgt Art. 64 mit den Worten: Les Articles compris sous le titre de dispositions particulières dans l'acte de la Confédération Germanique, tel qu'il se trouve annexé en original, et dans une traduction française, au présent traité général, auront la même force et valeur que s'ils étaient texuellement insérés ici. Art. 14 bildet demgemäß auch einen Bestandteil der Wiener Kongreßakte. Daraus folgt rückwärts: auch die deutsche Bundesakte erblickt das Hauptsächliche am Wesen der mittelbar gewordenen vormaligen reichsständischen Häuser nicht darin, daß sie vormals reichsständisch, sondern darin, daß sie vormals landesherrlich gewesen sind. Aus diesem Grunde, weil sie souverän gewesen waren, Souveränitätsrechte, „Staatsgewalt", „höhere Regierungsrechte" (Art. 14 c) besessen hatten, räumt ihnen die Bundesakte bevorrechtigte Untertanenstellung ein. Die Rheinbund-

akte von 1806 hat vorwiegend Länder reichsständischer Fürsten und Grafen den Staaten der Rheinbundesfürsten einverleibt. Trotzdem bezeichnet sie diese unterworfenen Fürsten und Grafen in dem Artikel, in welchem ihnen ein Teil ihrer Rechte erhalten, d. h. eine bevorzugte Untertanenstellung zugebilligt wird, nicht als bislang oder derzeit noch reichsständisch, sondern — in Artikel 27 — als actuellement regnans, d. h. als derzeit „regierend". Weil sie bislang „regierten", werden ihnen nun als Untertanen gewisse Vorrechte bewahrt. Die bayerische Deklaration vom 19. März 1807, welche die Stellung dieser Fürsten und Grafen, soweit ihre Länder mit Bayern verbunden wurden, näher geregelt hat, nennt sich „Deklaration die Bestimmung der künftigen Verhältnisse der der k. Souveränität unterworfenen Fürsten, Grafen und Herren zu den verschiedenen Zweigen der Staatsgewalt betreffend". Die der Kongreßakte angehängte Übersetzung des besonderen Teiles der Bundesakte gibt die Worte „Recht der Ebenbürtigkeit in dem bisher damit verbundenen Begriff" durch die Wendung wieder: droits d'égalité de naissance avec les maisons „souveraines" comme elles en ont joui jusqu'ici. Die Fürsten und Grafen, deren Gebiete den Ländern der Rheinbundesfürsten einverleibt waren, wurden allgemein als Mediatisierte bezeichnet (s. Georg Meyers Lehrbuch des deutschen Staatsrechts, 7. Aufl., bearbeitet von Anschütz 1914, § 36). So erklärt sich, daß der Ausdruck auch beibehalten wurde, als die zu verleihende Vorrechtsstellung nicht wie bei der Errichtung des Rheinbundes nur von dem bisherigen Besitze der Landesherrlichkeit, sondern dazu von dem Besitze der Reichsstandschaft abhängig gemacht wurde. Trotzdem blieb der Ausdruck Mediatisierte. Er wurde zum Wechsel-, zum abgekürzten Ausdruck für „mittelbar gewordene", für „mediatisierte vormalige Reichsstände". Wir sehen es in der Wiener Kongreß-, wir sehen es aber auch in der deutschen Bundesakte und zwar — ein schlagenderer Beweis läßt sich gar nicht denken — gerade an dem Artikel, der sedes materiae ist, an Art. 14. Im ersten Absatz von Art. 14 heißt es: die Bundesstaaten vereinigen sich zu gewissen Befugnis-Einräumungen, um den im Jahre 1806 und seitdem „mittelbar gewordenen ehemaligen Reichsständen" und Reichsangehörigen in Gemäßheit der gegenwärtigen Verhältnisse in allen Bundesstaaten einen gleichförmig bleibenden Rechtszustand zu verschaffen. In Absatz 2 wird dazu weiter verfügt: „Bei der näheren Bestimmung sowohl, wie überhaupt in allen übrigen Punkten wird zur weiteren Begründung und Feststellung eines in allen deutschen Bundesstaaten übereinstimmenden Rechtszustandes der „mittelbar gewordenen Fürsten, Grafen und Herren" die in dem Betreff erlassene Königlich Bayerische Verordnung vom Jahre 1807 als Basis und Norm unterlegt werden". In der französischen Übersetzung steht für mittelbar geworden: „mediatisiert".

B. Da somit nach dem Wortlaute von Bundes- und Kongreßakte mediatisierter Reichsfürst die Abkürzung für mediatisierter reichsständischer Fürst ist, liegt es nahe, daß die Vertragsteile von 1815 die bevorzugte Untertanenstellung auch solchen Fürsten zuerkannten, die im Jahre 1806 und seitdem ihre Landeshoheit verloren hatten, ohne reichsständisch gewesen zu sein. Weil nach der geschichtlichen Entwickelung — siehe Rheinbund — der Hauptgrund für das Belassen und Einräumen gewisser Vorrechte die Entziehung der Staatlichkeit war, läßt sich leicht verstehen, daß die Vertragsstaaten auch bereit waren, solchen Fürstlichkeiten die gleiche Rechtsstellung einzuräumen, die bei der Auflösung des Reiches nur eine Landeshoheit, aber keine Reichsstandschaft verloren.

1. Ein solcher Fürst war der Herzog von Croy. Er ist 1806 durch Unterordnung unter den Herzog von Arenberg der Landeshoheit über die Herrschaft Dülmen verlustig gegangen, die nie reichsständisches Gebiet gewesen war. Seine Rechtsstellung bezüglich Dülmen im Bunde wurde in Art. 43 der Kongreßakte geregelt. Es geschah zusammen mit der Ordnung der Rechtsverhältnisse einiger anderer Gebiete. Mit ihnen teilte Dülmen die Eigenschaft, daß sie alle zwischen 1806 und 1810 mediatisiert waren und 1815 durch Untergang der Staatsgewalt, der sie damals angehörten (Großherzogtum Berg, französische Departements in Deutschland) einen neuen Landesherrn, nämlich Preußen, erhielten. Auch waren unter den Ländern solche, auf denen keine Reichsstandschaft geruht hatte, die deshalb ebenso wie Dülmen niemals reichsständischen Charakter besessen hatten (so z. B. Steinfurt und Rheda). Aber immer handelte es sich um Gebiete, deren Inhaber anderwärts ehemals reichsständische Landesteile besaßen. Dülmen allein war ein Gebiet, dessen Herr auch keine anderweitigen Besitzungen hatte, die reichsständisch gewesen waren. Dülmen allein war ein mediatisierter Distrikt, dessen Eigentümer nirgends Reichsstandschaft besessen hatte. Für seinen Besitzer handelte es sich daher bei Erteilung der Privilegien des Art. 14 der Bundesakte nicht nur um Erstreckung, räumliche Erweiterung gegebener Voraussetzungen, sondern um Gewährung von Vorrechten trotz fehlender Voraussetzung, um Gleichstellung mit ehemaligen Reichsständen trotz Fehlens reichsständischer Eigenschaft nach jeder Richtung. Immerhin erfolgte die Gleichstellung. Der Rechtssatz lautet: Folgender mediatisierter Distrikt, die Besitzung, die der Herzog von Croy durch den Reichsdeputations-Hauptbeschluß vom 25. Februar 1803 im ehemaligen Kreise

Westfalen erhalten hat, wird in die Verhältnisse zum Königreich Preußen gestellt, welche die deutsche Bundesakte für die mediatisierten Territorien regeln wird. Die Herrschaft Dülmen ist deshalb in bezug auf die Privilegien des Art. 14 den mediatisierten vormals reichsständischen Territorien gleichgestellt, sie ist durch Kongreßakte Art. 43 zu einem mediatisierten ehemals reichsständischen Gebiet im Sinne des Art. 14 der Bundesakte erklärt.

2. Eine besondere Begünstigung lag darin noch aus folgendem Grunde. Dülmen war 1806 durch die Rheinbundesakte dem Herzog von Arenberg unterworfen worden. Dieser verlor seinerseits 1810 die Souveränität, indem seine Herrschaftsgebiete, also auch Dülmen, dem französischen Lippedepartement einverleibt wurden. Als diese Staatsgewalt 1815 ihr Ende erreichte und der in Westfalen gelegene Teil früheren Arenbergischen Herrschaftsgebietes, darunter Dülmen, unter preußische Staatshoheit gelangte, konnte die Frage entstehen, ob die Herrschaft Dülmen im Sinne der deutschen Bundesakte nicht als Besitzung des Herzogs von Arenberg anzusehen sei, der die Herrschaft seit 1806 landesherrlich besessen hatte und vormals reichsständisch war. Die Vorrechte des Art. 14 oder wenigstens ein Teil davon hätten dann für Dülmen dem Herzog von Arenberg zugestanden. Die Kongreßakte sprach sie ausschließlich dem Herzog von Croy zu.

Diese Begünstigung erfuhr das Haus Croy nicht allein. Die gleiche ward für die Herrschaft Gehmen (s. Klüber a. a. O. S. 888 u. 895) dem Freiherrn von Bömmelberg zuteil. Gehmen war reichsständisches Gebiet, 1806 kam es unter die Staatshoheit von Salm-Kyrburg. Dessen Gebiet wurde 1810 durch Einverleibung in den französischen Staat mediatisiert. Daher war die Frage, da Gehmen so doppelt mediatisiert war, ob es im Sinne von Bundesakte Art. 14 nicht als ehemals salmkyburgische Besitzung anzusehen sei. Die Kongreßakte Art. 14 entschied zugunsten des ehemaligen Reichsstandes Bömmelberg.

Eine Begünstigung hatte aber die Herrschaft Dülmen allein, die, daß sie die Vorrechte des Art. 14 erhielt, obwohl ihrem Besitzer jegliche Reichsstandschaft mangelte. Wegen ihrer mußte der Begriff des Mediatisierten, des Standesherrn im Sinne der deutschen Bundesakte gleich von Anfang an dahin definiert werden: Mediatisierte, Standesherren im Sinne der deutschen Bundesakte sind Besitzer von ehemaliger deutscher Landeshoheit und in der Regel auch ehemaliger deutscher Reichsstandschaft, die zwischen 1806 und 1815 der Staatsgewalt eines anderen deutschen Staates unterworfen wurden. Klüber § 301 definiert sie zutreffend als vormals deutsche „fast“ durchgehends reichsständische Landesherren, welche bei dem Fall der deutschen Reichsverbindung oder späterhin der Staatshoheit deutscher Souveräne untergeordnet wurden. Bis auf eine Ausnahme war Voraussetzung des Begriffes auch die Reichsstandschaft. Diese Ausnahme fand sich bei dem herzoglichen Hause Croy.

C. Noch sind drei Bedenken zu überwinden.

1. Erstens wird gesagt, weder der Wiener Kongreß noch der Deutsche Bund besaß gesetzgebende Gewalt. Deshalb konnten weder Kongreß noch Bund den Herzog von Croy zum deutschen Standesherren machen, ihn mit Wirkung für ganz Deutschland den mediatisierten ehemaligen Reichsständen gleichstellen, ihn für einen mittelbar gewordenen vormaligen Reichsstand erklären. Es ist möglich, daß ihn jeder Einzelstaat für sein Gebiet gleichstellt, daß ihn Preußen zum preußischen, Bayern zum bayerischen Standesherren erklärt, aber Standesherr für ganz Deutschland, deutscher Standesherr im Rechtssinne konnte er 1815 nicht werden. Dazu fehlte eine deutsche gesetzgebende Gewalt.

Diese Behauptung schießt über das Ziel. Nicht deutscher Standesherr im staatsrechtlichen Sinne, wohl aber deutscher Standesherr im Rechtssinne konnte der Herzog von Croy auch ohne eine deutsche gesetzgebende Gewalt werden. Rechtswirkung für ganz Deutschland wird auch durch rechtsnotwendig übereinstimmendes, d. h. auf völkerrechtlicher Bindung beruhendes, kraft völkerrechtlicher Verpflichtung ergangenes Landesrecht herbeigeführt. Es entspricht durchaus dem deutschen Sprachgebrauche und zwar auch dem der deutschen Rechtssprache, deutsch zu nennen, was auf vertraglich übereinstimmendem Landesrecht beruht. Eine deutsche Zollgemeinschaft kann sowohl auf Gesetz wie auf Vertrag beruhen. Deutsch wurde die Zollgemeinschaft der deutschen Staaten auch genannt, solange sie nur eine vertragsmäßige war. Sie trug allgemein den Namen Deutscher Zollverein. Der Bund der deutschen Staaten von 1815 hieß Deutscher Bund, hatte somit dieselbe Bezeichnung, wie zuerst (siehe Bundesgesetzblatt des Nordd. Bundes 1870 Nr. 51 S. 627, 650) das Deutsche Reich, obwohl das Recht dieses Bundes gegenüber den Untertanen nur übereinstimmendes Landes-, nicht übergeordnetes Einheitsrecht war. Wer bei vertraglich übereinstimmendem Recht aller deutschen Staaten die Beziehung Deutsch ablehnt, stellt die rechtliche Form über die rechtliche Wirkung. Dazu kommt aber: Art. 43 der Kongreßakte macht den Herzog von Croy in ganz derselben Rechtsform zum deutschen Standesherren, wie jeden mittelbar gewordenen Fürsten, der zugleich reichsständisch war. Die Bundesakte Art. 14 erklärt im Wege des Vertrages: mediatisierte Fürsten, die Reichsstände waren, sollen in allen deutschen Staaten privilegierte Untertanen sein, und Kongreßakte Art. 43 verfügt auf gleichen Wege: der mediatisierte Herzog von Croy soll in allen deutschen Staaten privilegierte Untertanenschaft besitzen. Der einzige formale Unterschied ist, daß die beiden Erklärungen äußerlich in verschiedenen Urkunden erfolgen: die erste Erklärung wird nur in der Bundesakte abgegeben. Allein dies ist bedeutungslos. Art. 14 der Bundesakte ist durch Art. 64 der Kongreßakte zum Textbestandteil der letzteren gemacht. Also sind die Mediatisierten des Art. 14 auch durch alle Vertragsstaaten als privilegierte anerkannt, Croy unmittelbar, sie zuerst durch die deutschen Bundesstaaten allein.

Nun kommt allerdings noch die staatsrechtliche Wirkung. Staatsrechtliche Wirkung soll die Privilegierung lediglich in allen Bundesstaaten haben. Aber auch diese ist da und dort in aller Form gegeben. Beide Verträge enthalten in das innere Staatsleben tief eingreifende Bestimmungen. Man denke bloß an die umfassenden Gebietsänderungen. Auch für Art. 14 der Bundes- und Art. 43 der Kongreßakte gilt dies. Hingewiesen sei in dieser Richtung nur auf die Bestimmung über den privilegierten Gerichtsstand, die Befreiung von aller Militärpflichtigkeit, das Recht des freien Aufenthaltes in jedem Bundesstaate und des freien Wegzuges nach jedem mit dem Bunde im Frieden lebenden Staate. Diese Bestimmungen bilden nach innen wichtige Vorschriften der Staatshäupter an ihre Behörden und Untertanen, also Gesetze. Durch den Abschluß der Verträge sind diese nicht erlassen, demgemäß Behörden und Volk nicht gebunden. Durch den Abschluß als solchen sind gebunden lediglich die Staaten untereinander. Die Mediatisierten haben durchaus noch kein Recht gegen Staat, Staatsorgane und Staatsuntertanen. Die Privilegien müssen ihnen erst verliehen, die Vorrechte erst durch Spezialgesetz geschaffen werden. Eher erzeugt der Inhalt der Verträge im Staatsinnern weder Rechte noch Pflichten. Aber dazu bedarf es nicht des Erlasses besonderer Gesetze neben den Verträgen. Es genügt, wenn die Verträge zugleich als Gesetze ergehen. Dazu gehört zu jener Zeit lediglich, daß sie im Staatsinnern irgendwie verkündet werden. Die deutschen Bundesstaaten waren 1815 zum größten Teil absolut oder, soweit sie ständische Verfassung besaßen, bedurfte es doch der Mitwirkung der Stände nicht, weil es sich um Privilegienverleihung handelte und die Privilegienverleihung zu den vom Landesherrn allein auszuübenden Hoheitsbefugnissen, zu seinen Vorbehaltsrechten zählte. Und was die Verkündigung betrifft, so war eine bestimmte Veröffentlichungsform nicht notwendig. Jedes gehörige Bekanntmachen an Behörden und Untertanen reichte hin. Durch jede solche Bekanntmachung waren die Privilegien verliehen, die Vorrechte begründet. Die Verkündigung in Gesetzblättern war zur verpflichtenden Kraft noch nicht erforderlich. In Preußen z. B. bestimmt erst ein Gesetz vom 3. April 1846, daß landesherrliche Erlasse, die Gesetzkraft erhalten sollen, sie nur durch Aufnahme in die Gesetzessammlung erlangen. Es gab in den Staaten 1815 bereits Verkündigungsblätter für landesherrliche Erlasse, Gesetzessammlungen, Regierungsblätter. Aber in keinem dieser, weder in Preußen, in Bayern u. s. w. sind Kongreß- oder Bundesakte abgedruckt, obwohl sie das innere Staatsrecht der Staaten so stark berühren. Sie sind nur sonst irgendwie den Beteiligten, Mediatisierten, Behörden, einfachen Untertanen kund gemacht, durch Abdruck in irgendwelchen Nachrichten oder durch irgendwelche sonstige ihr Ziel erreichende Mitteilung. Wohl sind in den Staaten Verordnungen, Deklarationen oder sonstige Erlasse der Landesherren über die Verhältnisse der Mediatisierten im Staate ergangen, so für Preußen die landesherrliche, in der Gesetzessammlung 1815 S. 105 publizierte vom 21. Juni 1815, aber keineswegs zur Einführung d. h. staatsrechtlichen Inkraftsetzung von Bundesakte Art. 14 und Kongreßakte Art. 43, sondern lediglich zur Ausführung und Ergänzung dieser Bestimmungen, als Ausführungsordnungen oder Ausführungsgesetze in Gemäßheit von Bundesakte Art. 14 Abs. 2, somit zur „näheren" Bestimmung der Vorrechte und zur „weiteren" Begründung und Feststellung eines übereinstimmenden Rechtszustandes in allen Bundesstaaten. Daß diese besonderen Erlasse zur Inkraftsetzung der Art. 14 und 43, daher zur Privilegienverleihung nicht erforderlich waren, zeigt nichts besser als die Tatsache, daß derartige Verordnungen nur in den Bundesstaaten ergingen, in denen Standesherrschaften lagen. Aufenthalts- und Wegzugsfreiheit und andere persönliche Rechte erwarben sie aber in allen Bundesstaaten, somit ohne besondere Verordnung, allein durch ausreichende Kundmachung von Bundes- und Kongreßakte innerhalb jedes einzelnen Staates. Selbst heute, wo die innerstaatliche Inkraftsetzung von Staatsverträgen, die wichtige Rechtsvorschriften enthalten, also nach innen Gesetze sind, nicht nur der Mitwirkung der Parlamente, sondern auch der Kundmachung durch das Gesetzblatt bedürfen, wird diese Art der Veröffentlichung in der Staatspraxis mehr oder weniger nicht angewendet oder abgewandelt. Das Staatsgewohnheitsrecht sieht alle Staatsverträge heute noch als Akte der Vollziehung, als Exekutivakte an, demgemäß auch solche, die Gesetze enthalten, also Gesetze in Vertragsform sind. So kommt vor, daß ihr Wortlaut oder wenigstens ihre Kündigung oder Verlängerung nicht im Gesetzblatt, sondern bloß in einem sonstigen amtlichen Blatte, dem Staats- oder Reichsanzeiger, kundgemacht wird. Vergl. Fleischmann, Art. Staatsverträge in Fleischmann, Wörterbuch des deutschen Staats- und Verwaltungsrechts 3. Bd. 1914 S. 514.

Die Richtigkeit der hier vertretenen Ansicht wird in jeder Beziehung bestätigt durch die Praxis des deutschen Bundes nach 1815. Die Bundesversammlung hat nachmals einigen Häusern die Vorrechte des Art. 14 zugesprochen, bei denen die Voraussetzungen dieses Artikels teilweise fehlten. Die Beschlüsse sind innerhalb der Staaten nicht durch Gesetzblätter, sondern sonst kundgemacht worden. Was die verbündeten Regierungen später durch kundgemachten völkerrechtlichen Beschluß vermochten, das konnten sie auch anfangs durch irgendwie publiziertes völkerrechtliches Abkommen. Und dann waren die Familien, die den vormals reichsständischen und seit 1806 mittelbar gewordenen Häusern später gleichgestellt wurden, vorwiegend Personalisten, d. h. solche, bei denen Reichsstandschaft vorhanden, Landeshoheit aber abwesend und deshalb eine Mediatisierung im eigentlichen Sinne unmöglich gewesen war (Schliz, Platen-Hallermund, Neipperg). Beim Hause Croy handelt es sich um eine Familie, die Realist war, d. h. Landeshoheit vor 1806 besessen und bis dahin nicht Reichsstandschaft erreicht hatte. Beim Hause Croy fehlte somit nicht das Merkmal, um dessenwillen in erster Linie die Bundesstaaten den mediatisierten Reichsständen eine Vorrechtsstellung zusprachen. Wenn Geschlechter gleichgestellt wurden, bei denen es an diesem wichtigsten Erfordernisse mangelte, dann ging es um so mehr rechtlich an, eine Familie gleichzuordnen, bei der diese Bedingung gegeben war.

2. Ein anderes Bedenken ist dieses. Kongreßakte Art. 43 bestimmt: der mediatisierte Distrikt, den der Herzog von Croy 1803 erhalten hat, wird in die Verhältnisse, welche die Bundesakte für die mittelbar gewordenen Territorien regelt, zur preußischen Monarchie gestellt. Das könnte wörtlich so verstanden werden, als sollte damit gesagt sein: der Distrikt Dülmen erhält die Privilegien des Art. 14 nur für den Bereich des Königreichs Preußen zuerkannt. Allein wie sowohl im Abs. 1 wie im Abs. 2 des Art. 14 bekundet wird, ist die erste Absicht der Regelung in Artikel 14, bezüglich der Mediatisierten für alle deutschen Bundesstaaten den gleichen Rechtszustand herzustellen, somit auch für die Staaten, in denen keine mediatisierten Gebiete sich befinden. Da sie in dieselben Verhältnisse zu Preußen gestellt werden soll, welche die Bundesakte für die mediatisierten Territorien regelt, wird die Herrschaft Dülmen durch Kongreßakte Art. 43 zu Preußen auch in das Verhältnis gebracht, welche die deutsche Bundesakte für die in Preußen belegenen Standesherrschaften in ihrer Beziehung zu andern deutschen Staaten regelt. Der Rechtssatz, daß Dülmen für die in Art. 14 geord-

neten Verhältnisse zu Preußen in Beziehung gestellt wird, will besagen, Preußen soll im Sinne der deutschen Bundesakte Art. 14 der Staat sein, zu dem die Standesherrschaft „gehört“ (Art. 14, Abs. 1 Buchstabe b), der Staat, in Beziehung zu welchem Dülmen als unterworfen, als mittelbar geworden gilt. Diese Bestimmung war für die in Art. 43 genannten Distrikte erforderlich, weil die Staaten, denen sie unterworfen wurden, als sie ihre Unmittelbarkeit einbüßten, andere waren, als das Königreich Preußen. Salm-Salm, Salm-Kyrburg wurden, als sie ihre Staatlichkeit verloren, dem Staate Frankreich, Rheina-Wolbeck (dem Herzog von Looz-Corswarem gehörig), Steinfurt, Recklinghausen, Rheda, Neustadt und Gimborn, Homburg dem Großherzogtum Berg, Rittberg dem Königreich Westfalen, Gehmen dem Fürstentume Salm-Kyrburg einverleibt. Das ist der Erforschung des wirklichen Willens entsprechend der Sinn der Worte: avec la monarchie Prusienne. In Art. 32 steht ebenso: avec le royaume Hanovre. Von den dort genannten Gebieten war der 1815 an Hannover gefallene Teil von Rheina-Wolbeck seinerzeit dem Großherzogtum Berg, Meppen 1810 dem Staate Frankreich zugeschlagen worden. Es hieße den Buchstaben über den Sinn stellen, wollte man behaupten, für die in Art. 32 und 43 genannten Gebiete sollen die Privilegien des Art. 14 lediglich im Verhältnis zu Preußen anerkannt werden. Die meisten dieser Gebiete waren reichsunmittelbar und reichsständisch. Es ist kein Grund ersichtlich, warum sie schlechter gestellt sein sollten, als die reichsständischen Territorien, die bereits bei ihrer Mediatisierung unter die Gewalt des deutschen Bundesstaates kamen, dem sie bei der Gründung des deutschen Bundes zugehörten.

Abgesehen davon verbietet der Zusammenhang eine solche Auslegung. Würde das in die Verhältnisse zu Preußen bzw. zu Hannover stellen in Art. 43 und 32 einschränkend auszulegen sein, so müßte das nämliche für Art. 52 geschehen. Dort ist betont: la principauté d'Isenbourg est placée sous la souveraineté de Sa M. J. et R. A. (l'Autriche) et sera envers Elle dans les rapports que la constitution fédérative de l'Allemagne règlera pour les états médiatisés. Das Fürstentum Isenburg soll also gegenüber dem Kaiser von Österreich in den Beziehungen sein, welche die Bundesakte für die mediatisierten Reichsstände regelt. Das Fürstentum war bis 1815 souverän. Sein Gebiet lag weit entfernt von Österreich, nahe Hessen und Kurhessen. Wie wäre da anzunehmen, daß das Fürstentum nur innerhalb Österreichs bevorrechtigt worden wäre. Jedenfalls hier bedeutet das „gegenüber dem Kaiser“: Österreich soll der Staat sein, dem das nun mediatisierte Fürstentum im Sinne der Bundesakte Art. 14 zugehört, in dem die Standesherrschaft liegt. Dann kann aber in Art. 43 wegen der weitgehenden Ähnlichkeit der

Wendungen (hier: sera envers Elle dans les rapports, dort: seront placés avec la monarchie Prusienne) die Erwähnung des Staates ebenfalls nichts anderes besagen als Staat, zu dem das standesherrliche Gebiet gehört. Die Staatenpraxis ist in all den Fällen richtig verfahren. Die durch Art. 32, 43, 52 privilegierten Standesherrschaften wurden sämtlich auch von denjenigen Bundesstaaten, in denen sie nicht belegen sind, als Vorzüge mit sich bringende Besitzungen anerkannt. Das zeigt besonders augenfällig die Tatsache, daß auch andere Staaten, als die der belegenen Standesherrschaft an die standesherrlichen Häupter das Prädikat Durchlaucht und Erlaucht verliehen. S. darüber Rehm, Prädikat und Titelrecht §§ 11 ff.; auch das Verzeichnis der deutschen Standesherren bei Klüber a. a. O. Anhang IV und bei Fleischmann Art. Mediatisierte in dessen angeführten Wörterbuch Bd. 2, (1913) S. 830.

3. Und endlich das dritte Bedenken. Veranlaßt durch die Ausführungen von Dresch von den Rechtsverhältnissen der Standesherren in dessen Abhandlungen (1830) S. 129 hat das Landgericht zu Münster in Westfalen in einem Rechtsstreite des Hauses Croy am 13. Januar 1904 über das Verhältnis von Bundesakte Art. 14 zu Kongreßakte Art. 43 und 32 ausgesprochen: Es springt sofort als Unterschied zwischen diesen Bestimmungen und denen des Art. 14 in die Augen, daß hier, d. h. in Art. 43 und 32 nur von Territorien, dem Land, dort aber von den fürstlichen Häusern und ihren Verhältnissen die Rede ist. Daraus wird gefolgert: Die Besitzer der in Art. 32 und 43 genannten Gebiete sind als solche nur Inhaber der territorialen, nicht auch der persönlichen Vorrechte, die Art. 14 der Bundesakte verleiht, insbesondere daher nicht ebenbürtig.

Diese Auslegung scheitert schon am Wortlaut der in Betracht kommenden Bestimmungen. In dem ganzen Art. 14 der Bundesakte befindet sich nicht das Wort Territorien. Es ist dort auch in der französischen Übersetzung allein die Rede von Besitzungen, Eigentum, Gütern (possessions, propriétés, biens). Deshalb muß aus Art. 14 dasjenige Wort zum Vergleiche herangezogen werden, das dem Worte Territorium entspricht, und das ist der „mittelbar gewordene Reichsstand“, der „mittelbar gewordene Fürst, Graf, Herr“. Die Verhältnisse dieser, also der Territorial- oder Landesherren hat der Art. 14 geregelt, und daß diese auch in der Kongreßakte mit Territorien gemeint sind, zeigt der Zusatz mediatisiert. Mediatisiert steht in der französischen Übersetzung des Art. 14 bei Reichsstand, Fürsten, Grafen, Herren. Die Verhältnisse und Beziehungen, die in dem Sinne der Kongreßakte durch die Bundesakte für die mediatisierten Territorien geregelt sind und in denen sich jedes der in Art. 32 und 43 genannten Gebiete gegenüber dem Staate, dem es einverleibt wird, befinden wird (Art. 32: se trouvera envers le royaume d'Hanovre dans la relations que la constitution fédérative de l'Allemagne règlera pour les territoires médiatisés), sind deshalb, um Worte des Art. 14 zu gebrauchen, die Verhältnisse der mediatisierten Herren „in Rücksicht ihrer Personen, Familien und Besitzungen". Was in Art. 14 für die mediatisierten Territorien geregelt wird, sind die Verhältnisse der Personen, Familien und Besitzungen ihrer Herren. Demgemäß sind auch die Verhältnisse, in welche die in Kongreßakte Art. 43 genannten mediatisierten Distrikte gegenüber Preußen gestellt werden, die Verhältnisse der Personen, Familien und Besitzungen der mediatisierten Herren, somit auch die diesen zuerkannten persönlichen Vorrechte, demgemäß auch das der Ebenbürtigkeit.

Zu dem gleichen Ergebnis führt der Zusammenhang der Kongreßakte. In Art. 52 bringt sie die Bestimmung gleichen Inhalts, wie Art. 32 und 43, für das Fürstentum Isenburg. Hier steht statt: „règlera pour les territoires médiatisés": règlera pour les états médiatisés; d. h. mediatisierte Reichsstände. Mediatisiertes Territorium und Mediatisierter Reichsstand sind daher in der Kongreßakte Wechselausdrücke. In Art. 43 darf deshalb gelesen werden: Verhältnisse, welche die Bundesakte für die mediatisierten Reichsstände regeln wird; für sie hat die Akte auch solche ihrer Personen und ihrer Familien geordnet.

Die Praxis der Bundesstaaten hat darum mit Recht allen Besitzern der in Art. 32 und 43 genannten Distrikte im Staate des Distrikts — und ebenso anderwärts — ohne Ausnahme auch die Vorrechte eingeräumt, welche die Bundesakte den mittelbar gewordenen Reichsständen für Person und Familie zuspricht. Besonders zeigen dies die Ausführungsverordnungen zu den Bundesratsbeschlüssen über Durchlaucht und Erlaucht von 1825 und 1829.

II. Wir sahen, das Haus Croy besitzt das Recht der Ebenbürtigkeit. Nicht dagegen besitzt es die Pflicht der Ebenbürtigkeit, d. h. nicht hat es die Pflicht, nur solche Ehen seiner Mitglieder als die Ebenbürtigkeit mit den souveränen Häusern forterhaltend anzusehen, welche seine Mitglieder mit standesgleichen Personen schließen.

Zunächst zeigt diese Gegenüberstellung von Recht und Pflicht der Ebenbürtigkeit, daß das Wort Ebenbürtigkeit beide Male nicht ganz dasselbe bedeutet. Beim „Rechte" ist der Begriff enger. Hier bedeutet es Standesgleichheit mit den regierenden Häusern. Die Bundesakte sagt: „Recht der Ebenbürtigkeit in dem „bisher" damit verbundenen Begriff"; d. h. die mediatisierten Fürsten behalten, trotzdem sie nicht mehr regieren, gleichen Stand mit den regierenden Fürsten. Im zweiten Falle bedeutet Ebenbürtigkeit schlechthin Standesgleichheit. Dort bedeutet das Gegenteil unebenbürtig den Regierenden, hier unebenbürtig dem standesherrlichen Hause. Standesgleichheit mit den souveränen Häusern ist hier nicht gefordert. Um die Standesgleichheit mit ihnen zu bewahren, ist nicht notwendig, daß die Mitglieder der mediatisierten Familien nur Ehen mit Angehörigen souveräner Geschlechter eingehen.

Im übrigen sagen wir: Diese Pflicht der Ebenbürtigkeit besteht für das Haus Croy überhaupt nicht.

A. An sich ist das Gegenteil der Fall. Infolge ihrer Gleichstellung mit den mittelbar gewordenen reichsständischen Häusern ist die Familie Croy 1815 Mitglied des hohen Adels in Deutschland geworden. Demgemäß trat für sie 1815 das gemeine Privatfürstenrecht in Kraft, aber seiner Natur gemäß nur hilfsweise, daher bloß soweit, als sich im Hause Croy nicht besonders Hausrecht bildete. Nach gemeinem Privatfürstenrecht war damals wie auch heute noch die Ehe einer Person des hohen Adels mit einer bürgerlichen Person unter allen Umständen eine notorische Mißheirat, daher keine standesgleiche Ehe, aber ebenso gewiß konnte im einzelnen Hause nach besonderem Privatfürstenrecht der Satz gelten, daß die fürstenrechtliche Ehe nicht standesgleich, nicht ebenbürtig zu sein braucht, daß also auch unebenbürtige Ehen standesgemäß, fürstenrechtsgemäß, fürstenrechtlich gültig sind. Vgl. Schücking Art. Ebenbürtigkeit in Fleischmanns Wörterbuch des deutschen Staats- und Verwaltungsrechts Bd. 1 (1911) S. 626; Meyer-Anschütz, Lehrb. des deutschen Staatsrecht, 7. Aufl. 1914, § 89 S. 299; Emil Abt, Mißheiraten in den deutschen Fürstenhäusern unter besonderer Berücksichtigung der standesherrlichen Familien in den „Deutschrechtlichen Beiträgen“ hsgeg. von K. Beyerle, Bd. VII (1912) S. 138.

Im Hause Croy hat von dem Augenblicke an, wo es deutschhochadelig wurde, demgemäß von 1815 ab, privatfürstliches Sonderrecht gegolten. Dies ergibt sich auf folgende Weise.

1. Die Familie Croy wurde erst 1815 hochadelig in Deutschland, aber schon vorher hatte sie einmal eine Sonderstellung in Deutschland besessen. Sie war von 1803 bis 1806 regierend. Dies bedeutete Erwerb von Autonomie. Die Satzungsgewalt der deutschen Reichsstände war kein Ausfluß der Reichsstandschaft, sondern der Landeshoheit. In der Landeshoheit liegt die geschichtliche Wurzel der Autonomie. S. Edgar Löning, Die Autonomie der standesherrlichen Häuser Deutschlands nach dem Rechte der Gegenwart (nicht im Buchhandel) 1905, S. 23 ff. Den besten Beweis hiefür liefert die Tatsache, daß Absatz 3 von Art. 14

der deutschen Bundesakte die Autonomie auch des niederen deutschen Reichsadels aufrecht erhielt. Wenn die Reichsritter Satzungsgewalt besaßen, so konnte der Grund nur in der Reichsunmittelbarkeit, also in ihrer obrigkeitlichen Stellung, in ihren Herrschaftsrechten enthalten sein, denn Sitz und Stimme auf dem Reichstag hatten sie nicht.

Als der Herzog von Croy 1803 Landesherr von Dülmen wurde, war die erste Frage, unter welches Recht die Nachfolge in die Landesherrlichkeit zu stehen kam. Im Lande selbst war eine besondere Ordnung hiefür nicht vorhanden. Denn Dülmen war kein Staat, sondern nur ein Staatsteil gewesen und obendrein der Teil eines geistlichen Fürstentums. Demgemäß galt an und für sich, daß das Land so vererbt, wie sich bisher Vermögen im Hause Croy vererbte. Dem Herzog von Croy war das Amt Dülmen zur Entschädigung zugeteilt, somit erblich, mit Erblichkeit in dem herzoglichen Hause. Unangebracht wäre der Einwand: bei der Nachfolge in die Herrschaft Dülmen handelte es sich nicht um Nachfolge im Vermögen, sondern um Nachfolge in Hoheit, somit nicht um Erbschaft im Sinne des privaten Erbrechts. Abgesehen davon, daß in jenem Zeitraume die Herrschaft über das Land noch als ein Stück Vermögen, als etwas vermögensähnliches und demgemäß die Nachfolge in die obrigkeitliche Stellung als Nachfolge in eine Verlassenschaft, als Nachfolge in die Staatsverlassenschaft angesehen wurde, enthielt die Landesherrlichkeit auch Vermögensrechte, die alle, weil man zwischen privaten und öffentlichen Vermögensrechten noch nicht scharf schied, als Gegenstand der privatrechtlichen Erbschaft angesehen wurden. Die Nachfolge in die Landesherrlichkeit war Nachfolge in Regierungs- und Vermögens-, d. h. auch Eigentums- und Nutzungsrechte. Somit lag nahe, daß die Landeshoheit so vererbte, wie Vermögen im Hause Croy.

Welches Recht in der Familie Croy gegolten hatte und wie der ganze Entwicklungsgang war, ist gut geschildert und läßt sich gut entnehmen aus einem Schreiben des Herzogs von Croy an den Oberpräsidenten der Provinz Westfalen Freiherrn von Vincke vom 10. Juni 1841. Es war veranlaßt durch eine amtliche Zuschrift dieses Herrn vom 2. Juni 1841, die darauf hinweist, wie notwendig es sei, daß die standesherrlichen Besitzungen nicht durch Wegverkauf verringert und zersplittert würden.

In dem Geschlechte der Croy hat nach altem, unbestrittenem Herkommen die Bestimmung bestanden, daß sich die Besitzungen des Hauses ungeteilt nach dem Rechte der Erstgeburt in absteigender Linie vererben, es also ein Pflichtteilsrecht der Nachgeborenen daran nicht gab. M. a. W.: Die Güter waren gebunden und zwar fideikommissarisch gebunden. Allein dieses Erbrecht galt im Hause Croy nicht mehr, als der Herzog Dülmen erwarb. Die bisherigen Besitzungen des Hauses lagen in Frankreich und den Niederlanden (Belgien). Dort war inzwischen jenes Erbfolgerecht außer Kraft getreten. Die Revolution hat in Frankreich 1792 die Gebundenheit des Besitzes, das Fideikommiß, aufgehoben und für alle Güter gewöhnliches Erbrecht, also auch Pflichtteilsrecht eingeführt. Dasselbe geschah in den Niederlanden. Diese haben sich 1795 als Batavische Republik verfaßt. Die neue Republik hat die umstürzlerischen Einrichtungen Frankreichs bis ins kleinste nachgeahmt und deshalb ebenfalls die fideikommissarische Gebundenheit von Gütern beseitigt. So konnten Abweichungen vom Grundsatz der Gleichheit des Erbrechts lediglich durch Testament und Kodizill, immer aber nur unter Wahrung der Pflichtteilsansprüche der Nachgeborenen geschaffen werden.

Diesen Zustand fand der Herzog von Croy vor, als er das Amt Dülmen erwarb. Für die Nachfolge in die erworbene Herrschaft galt an sich dies neue Recht, das, was in Testamenten und Kodizillen über Vermögensnachfolge enthalten war. Aber er konnte auch neues Recht über die Nachfolge in die Herrschaft und Einkünfte des Landes Dülmen schaffen. Er konnte es kraft seiner neugewonnenen Staats- und Hausgewalt, kraft der ersteren für die Untertanen und zwar absolut, denn Landstände waren nicht vorhanden, kraft der letzeren für das Haus, für letztere allerdings nur, soweit er in erworbene Rechte der Agnaten, also Pflichtteilsrechte eingriff, unter deren Zustimmung. Er tat es, indem er für den neu erworbenen Besitz, die Herrschaft und die Einkünfte des Landes Dülmen, wieder die Nachfolgeordnung einführte, die im Hause Croy von altersher gegolten hatte, die Primogeniturordnung. Durch Erklärung vom 1. Oktober 1803 hat Anna Emmanuel, der erste regierende Herr des Hauses, alle bisherigen Testamente und Kodizille als den Zeitumständen nicht mehr angemessen aufgehoben. Die letztwillige Verfügung lautet: „Les circonstances ayant changés, j'annulle tous testamens et codicilles faits antérieurement à la date d'aujourd'hui. Und am 22. Oktober 1803 hat er durch Verordnung als eine „ewige und unabweichliche Richtschnur zur Befolgung für seine Landesnachfolger und die ganze herzogliche Familie", somit als Staats- und Familiengesetz die Primogeniturordnung eingeführt und dafür auch die Anerkennung der Agnaten erhalten, indem er an die Stelle der Pflichtteilsrechte der Nachgeborenen Apanagen für sie setzte. M. a. W.: Er hat das Land Dülmen und seine Einkünfte zum Staats- und Hausfideikommiß erklärt. S. über diese Ausdrücke Rehm, Die staatsrechtliche Stellung des Hauses Wittelsbach zu Bayern in Ver-

Die Verordnung vom 22. Oktober 1803 lautet in dem maßgebenden Teile: „Da zur besseren Aufrechterhaltung der regierenden Familien schier alle Fürsten Deutschlands die Primogenitur in ihren Staaten eingeführt haben, so soll selbe von nun an auch in Rücksicht des Landes Dülmen satthaben; dergestalt, daß immer der Erstgeborene des wirklichen Regenten und dessen weitere erstgeborene Söhne mit Ausschluß der übrigen so männlicher als weiblicher Deszendenz in die Regierung des Fürstentums Dülmen und dessen Einkünfte sukzedieren.“ Das „auch“ bedeutet: ebenso wie in den anderen Staaten Deutschlands; nicht auch: ebenso wie für die außerdeutschen Besitzungen des Hauses. Dieses scheint nach dem Wortlaut die Fideikommißurkunde des Enkels des Herzogs Anna Emmanuel vom 10. Februar 1860 zu meinen. Dort heißt es in der Einleitung: Durch die provisorische Verordnung vom 22. Oktober 1803 hatte mein Großvater die von altersher in meiner Familie bestandene Sukzessionsordnung nach dem Rechte der Erstgeburt „auch“ auf das meinem Hause zur Entschädigung angewiesene Amt Dülmen „übertragen“. Allein dieser Satz ist nicht rechtlich, sondern nur geschichtlich zu verstehen. Rechtlich bedeutet er nicht ein Übertragen, also ein Erstrecken, sondern ein Wiedereinführen. Der Grundsatz, der für die Besitzungen in Frankreich und Belgien seit langem galt, für sie aber aufgehoben ist, soll wieder aufleben im neuen Besitze des Hauses.

Mit dem Verluste der Landeshoheit im Jahre 1806 hat die Herrschaft Dülmen aufgehört, Staatsfideikommiß zu sein. Von da an ist sie nur mehr autonomes Hausfideikommiß. Auch diese Eigenschaft verlor sie, als Dülmen unter französische Staatshoheit gelangte. Hierdurch erlangten Fideikommiß- und demgemäß auch Erstgeburtrecht ihr Ende. Allein beides lebte mit Wiederherstellung deutscher Herrschaft wieder auf. Durch Art. 43 der Wiener Kongreßakte trat dann die hochadelige Eigenschaft hinzu. Dülmen, bisher nur autonomes Hausgut, ist jetzt hochadeliges autonomes Hausgut. Herzog Alfred von Croy gab ihm, es durch andere Besitzungen erweiternd, durch Urkunde vom 10. Februar 1860 eine neue Ordnung und dies neue Hausgesetz hat dann — nach Bestätigung durch das Appellationsgericht zu Münster als Fideikommißgericht am 17. April 1860 — unter dem 18. Juni 1860 gemäß § 21 der Instruktion vom 30. Mai 1821 die Genehmigung des Königs von Preußen erhalten. Anders ausgedrückt: Die Primogeniturordnung von 1803 ist 1815 hochadeliges Recht, also Privatfürstenrecht geworden und als solches 1860 durch die Fideikommißstiftungsurkunde von 1860 ersetzt worden. Wir haben deshalb seit 1815 ein besonderes Privatfürstenrecht des Hauses Croy.

B. Die Frage, die entsteht, ist die, ob dies besondere Privatfürstenrecht auch den Satz umfaßte, daß Ebenbürtigkeit keine Voraussetzung fürstenrechtlich gültiger Ehen in der Familie Croy bildet. In der Tat ist dies der Fall. Es war dies so nach dem Hausstatut von 1803 und es ist so geblieben nach dem Familiengesetze von 1860. Das hochadelige Haus Croy hat von dem Augenblicke an, wo es hochadelig wurde, eine besondere Nachfolgeordnung besessen und diese auch seither behalten und nach ihr bildet Ebenbürtigkeit keine Bedingung für eine Vollehe im hochadeligen Hause Croy.

1. Die Primogeniturordnung vom 22. Oktober 1803 bestimmt: in Rücksicht des Landes Dülmen soll von nun an die Primogenitur statthaben. Es fragt sich, unter wem soll das Erstgeburtsrecht gelten. Darauf antwortet die Ordnung: unter der regierenden Familie, unter der männlichen wie weiblichen Deszendenz. Die Verordnung sagt einmal: Die Primogenitur solle auch in Rücksicht des Landes statthaben, da schier alle Fürsten Deutschlands sie zur besseren Aufrechterhaltung „der regierenden Familien“ eingeführt haben, und dann bestimmt sie, die Primogenitur solle in Rücksicht des Landes Dülmen dergestalt gelten, daß immer der Erstgeborene des wirklichen Regenten und dessen weitere erstgeborenen Söhne, mit Ausschluß der übrigen so männlich als weiblichen Deszendenz in der Regierung des Fürstentums Dülmen und dessen Einkünften sukzedieren.

Unter den Angehörigen der regierenden Familie soll somit die Erstgeburtsordnung gelten. Wer ist diese regierende Familie? Die Verordnung nennt als sie die ganze herzoglich Croysche Familie. Die Verordnung beginnt mit den Worten: Wir von Gottes Gnaden Anna Emmanuel, des Heiligen Römischen Reiches Fürst, Herzog von Croy, als nunmehriger Fürst des Landes Dülmen verkünden und bekennen für Uns und Unsere Landes-Sukzessoren und Regenten, so wie auch „für die ganze Herzoglich Croysche Familie“. Die Verordnung fährt fort: wir haben folgendes als eine ewige und unabweichliche Richtschnur zur Befolgung für unsere Landes-Nachfolger und „die ganze Herzogliche Familie“ festgesetzt. Und die Verordnung schließt mit dem Satze: Zur Vorbeugung aller Zwistigkeiten und Mißverständnisse haben Wir Uns bewogen gefunden, vorläufig gegenwärtige provisorische Verordnung zur Richtschnur der „Familie“ zu errichten. Die Primogeniturordnung soll demgemäß gelten in der ganzen herzoglich Croyschen Familie. Das will nicht sagen: auch in der Seitenverwandtschaft des Herzogs Anna Emmanuel, die wir mit dem Gothaer Genealogischen Hofkalender, Jahrg. 1913 S. 122, kurz als die Linie Havré bezeichnen; sie soll nur gelten in der ganzen regierenden Linie, die wir kurz den

Zweig Solre nennen; sie soll nur gelten in dem Teil des damaligen Gesamthauses, der von dem ersten Erwerber der Landeshoheit abstammt. Aber immerhin soll die Ordnung gelten im herzoglichen Hause Croy, demgemäß unter denen, die Mitglieder dieses Hauses werden. Demgemäß haben das Sukzessionsrecht erworben, das „eventuelle" und das der Erstgeburt, die Mitglieder des Hauses Croy, die vom ersten Erwerber der Landeshoheit abstammen. Voraussetzung des Nachfolgerechts ist nur die Zugehörigkeit zum Hause Croy. Wie diese bisher erworben wurde, so soll sie weiter erworben werden. Das Geschlecht war bisher ein französisches. In Frankreich gilt nicht Ebenbürtigkeit. Demgemäß wurde Ebenbürtigkeit auch jetzt kein Nachfolgerechts-Erfordernis. Wohl haben sich die Angehörigen des Hauses bisher regelmäßig adelig verheiratet, aber daraus hatte sich kein Gewohnheitsrecht gebildet, es war Verkehrssitte im Hause, Hausüberlieferung, aber nicht Hausherkommen. Darum änderte sich die Rechtsordnung auch jetzt nicht. Die Eheschließungsübung hatte auch jetzt keine andere Wirkung, zumal die Hausmitglieder nach wie vor überwiegend Angehörige des französischen Adels ehelichten.

2. Das wird auch durch anderes bestätigt.

a) Zuvörderst blieben Titel und Wappen des regierenden Hauses die gleichen wie vorher.

α) Als der Herzog von Croy 1803 Teile des Amtes Dülmen zugesprochen erhielt, erwarb er einen deutschen Stand, aber keinen deutschen Titel. Er wurde regierender Herr in Deutschland, also deutscher Landesherr und damit deutscher Reichsfürst im weiteren Sinne des Wortes. Dülmen wurde Land und damit er Herr dieses Landes, Dülmen Fürstentum im weiteren Sinne und er Landesfürst. Aber der Herzog nahm von dieser seiner neuen Stellung nicht auch einen neuen Namen an. Er hätte nur „Herr von Dülmen" sein können. Denn Dülmen war nur Teil eines Amtes gewesen und wurde nicht zur Grafschaft oder zum Fürstentum erhoben. Es wurde somit nur deutsche Herrschaft und demgemäß der Erwerber der Landeshoheit innerhalb des Fürstenstandes weiteren Sinnes nur „Herr", nicht „Graf", nicht „Fürst". Der Reichsdeputations-Hauptschluß verlieh dem Herzog für Dülmen keine Virilstimme und um Aufnahme in das Grafenkollegium hatte er erst nachzusuchen. Der Titel, der erworben wurde, war deshalb nur Herr von Dülmen. Ihn vermied der Herzog. Er war zu niedrig. Deutlich zeigt das Ganze die Verordnung vom 22. Oktober 1803. Fürst von Dülmen durfte sich Anna Emmanuel nicht nennen, Herr von Dülmen wollte er sich nicht heißen. So nennt er sich nur: Fürst und Regent „des Landes" Dülmen. Sein Titel blieb Herzog von Croy. So der Eingang der Verordnung und so die Unterschrift („Anna Emmanuel Herzog von Croy").

Dieser Titel war aber kein deutscher. Er wurde nicht nostrifiziert, d. h. durch Anerkennung einem deutscher Verleihung gleichgestellt. Jede solche Urkunde fehlt, jetzt und später. Der Titel blieb demzufolge ein ausländischer und zwar einer französischer Verleihung. Vom König von Frankreich war er verliehen. Deshalb galt für ihn französisches Recht fort. Ihm gemäß galt für seine Vererbung Erstgeburt- und Lineal-Erbfolge — lediglich das Haupt hieß Herzog von Croy, die übrigen Mitglieder nur Prinz und Prinzessin —, dagegen nicht Ebenbürtigkeit, so wenig wie bei der königlichen Familie Frankreichs.

Daran änderte auch die Unterstellung unter Bundesakte Art. 15 nichts. Die Familie Croy erwarb dadurch einen neuen Stand, den des deutschen Hochadels und innerhalb desselben den eines ehemaligen, aber mediatisierten Reichsstandes, aber keinen neuen Titel. Der Titel blieb der alte; demgemäß für seinen Erwerb auch das alte Recht: Fehlen des Ebenbürtigkeitserfordernisses.

β) Und was für den Titel gilt, gilt auch für das Wappen. Wie die Herzoge von Croy keinen Titel annahmen, der ihre Beziehung zu Dülmen ausdrückt, so sah sich der Erwerber der Landeshoheit über Dülmen auch nicht veranlaßt, ein neues Wappen aufzunehmen oder dem alten, ausländischen, Abzeichen anzufügen, die auf den neuen Besitz hindeuten.

γ) Die Herzoge von Croy unterließen, als sie Landesherren wurden, neuen Titel und anderes Wappen anzustreben, obwohl darin eine Ursache gelegen hätte, daß von nun ab das Haus Croy in zwei rechtlich verschiedene Häuser, in ein regierendes und ein nichtregierendes Teilhaus, zerfiel. Trotzdem unterschied sich der Zweig Solre nicht vom Ast d'Havré. Das beweist, daß er für Titel und Wappen das alte Recht in Geltung erhalten wissen wollte.

b) Dann aber folgender Beweis. Die Primogeniturordnung von 1803 spricht von sehr vielen durch die Primogenitur veranlaßten Einrichtungen, von Aufhebung des Pflichtteils, Apanage, Morgengabe, Nadel-, Wittums- und Wiederkehr-Geldern, Aussteuer und Brautschatz. Hätte Ebenbürtigkeit eingeführt werden wollen, so würde dies deshalb auch ausdrücklich geschehen sein.

Hiergegen läßt sich nicht einwenden: das mag richtig sein, aber 1803 wurde das Haus noch nicht hochadelig; demgemäß galt für es damals noch nicht ohne weiteres gemeines Privatfürstenrecht; anders liegt es seit 1815. Dieser Einwand zerschellt an dem Umstande, daß wir derselben Erscheinung in dem Hausstatut von 1860, daher in einem

Hauserlasse begegnen, der aus der Zeit nach Erwerb des Hochadels stammt. Dieses Hausgesetz regelt die Nachfolge, die Vormundschaft über den Fideikommißbesitzer, den Eintritt seiner Großjährigkeit, die Erziehungsgelder und die Einkünfte des Besitzers vor seiner Selbständigkeit, also vor Antritt der eigenen Verwaltung, den Wohnort des Fideikommißinhabers, Wittum, Apanagen, Unterhaltsrenten, Aussteuer und Brautschatz der Mitglieder, und zwar im Gegensatz zur Verordnung von 1803 alles eingehend. Trotzdem fehlt sogar hier jede ausdrückliche Bemerkung über Ebenbürtigkeit. Bei dieser Sachlage kann das Schweigen über Ebenbürtigkeit nicht dahin ausgelegt werden, daß sie eben nach gemeinem Fürstenrecht seit 1815 von selbst galt und Herzog Alfred dies Recht einfach fortgelten lassen wollte. Dies anzunehmen verbieten eine Reihe anderer Gründe.

Erstens ist das Statut in einer Periode erlassen, wo die standesherrlichen Familien bereits begannen, das alte Prinzip des Fürstenrechtes, Bindung der fürstenrechtlichen Ehegültigkeit an Ebenbürtigkeit, zu verlassen und sich auf das formelle schon vorhandene oder neu eingeführte zu beschränken, auf das der Heiratsbewilligung des Familienhauptes. Fürstenrechtlich gültig, Vollehe, ist auch die Heirat mit Unebenbürtigen, wenn sie vom Haupt des Hauses genehmigt ist. So Castell (Hausgesetz v. 6. Juli 1827 u. 14. Juni 1861; s. bayer. Reg.-Blatt 1830 und 1864), Giech 1855 und seitdem Solms-Laubach 1894, Leiningen 1897.

Zweitens hat die Urkunde infolge einer allerdings nicht zu billigenden Auffassung des preußischen Justizministeriums zugleich die Form der Fideikommißstiftung; sie ist als solche auch vom Gericht verlautbart und bestätigt. Für die Fideikommißnachfolge genügt im Zweifel Abstammung aus jeder Ehe.

Drittens ist das Statut nach 1854 erlassen, demgemäß nach der Berufung des Hauptes der standesherrlichen Familie zum erblichen Mitglied des Herrenhauses. Die Berufung ist 1854 an den Herzog ergangen, also an den, dessen Titel sich nach dem Titel-Verleihungs-Dekret richtet, und dieses, vom französischen König stammend, kennt die Ebenbürtigkeit nicht als Voraussetzung des Titelerwerbs.

Ferner ist dann im Statute als nachfolgeberechtigt auch der Weibsstamm genannt.

Hierbei ist ein Doppeltes bemerkenswert. Einmal wird gesagt: derjenige vom Weibsstamm, auf den in solchem Falle das Fideikommiß übergeht, soll gehalten sein, Namen und Wappen der Familie Croy anzunehmen und zu führen. Es ist nicht anzunehmen, daß der Fideikommißstifter meint, daß dafür schwereres gelten soll, als nach dem

Gnadenakt des französischen Königs von 1788. Außerdem würde ein solcher Erwerb nur durch Verleihung seitens des Königs von Preußen geschehen können. Dieser hat die Herzöge von Croy unter Anerkennung ihres ausländischen Titels nach den Grundsätzen des Patentes von 1788 in das Herrenhaus berufen. Nicht wahrscheinlich ist, daß der Fideikommißstifter dem Könige ansinnen wollte, für den genannten Übergangsfall mehr Bedingungen zu machen.

Dazu kommt dann folgendes. Die Kognatenerbfolge ist besonders eingehend geregelt. Wir lesen: Ist der Mannesstamm des Stifters und seiner Brüder Ferdinand und Philipp erloschen, dann soll das Fideikommiß zur kognatischen Primogenitur auf die weibliche Linie zurückfallen, die vom Stifter und seiner männlichen (agnatischen) Nachkommenschaft abstammt, und zwar in der Art, daß alsdann auf die Erstgeburt im Verhältnis zum Fideikommißstifter behufs Feststellung der zur Sukzession gelangenden Linie und in dieser wieder auf die männliche Erstgeburt zur Feststellung der Erbfolgeberechtigung des einzelnen Mitgliedes gesehen werden soll. „Die Linie meiner ältesten Tochter schließt daher alle jüngeren Linien und in jeder älteren Linie der sich am nächsten zur Primogenitur ziehende Nebenast alle übrigen Zweige aus. In jeder Linie wird übrigens von der männlichen Deszendenz die weibliche ausgeschlossen. Wenn z. B. meine älteste Tochter mit Tod abgegangen, so fällt das Fideikommiß zunächst auf den ältesten ihrer Söhne und auf die männlichen Deszendenten desselben. Sind weder Söhne von ihr noch entfernte von diesen Söhnen in männlicher Linie abstammende Deszendenten vorhanden, so kommen die männlichen Deszendenten zunächst ihrer ältesten Tochter nach Anordnung der Erstgeburt zur Sukzession.“

Der Stifter nennt somit die Töchter sehr oft und zwar die ihm besonders nahestehenden, seine älteste und deren Söhne und Töchter. Deshalb ist davon auszugehen, daß ihm bei der Abfassung der Urkunde die Möglichkeit bewußt war, daß die Töchter des Hauses Unebenbürtige, insbesondere Bürgerliche heiraten. Nichtsdestoweniger kein Wort darüber, daß er der Möglichkeit vorbeugen will, daß das Fideikommiß an eine unebenbürtige, insbesondere eine bürgerliche Familie gelange.

Aber nicht nur hier, sondern auch bei anderen Bestimmungen wäre Veranlassung gewesen, die Ebenbürtigkeitsfrage zu berühren. Es wird gehandelt von Wittum, Apanage, Sustentation, von Agnaten, weiblichen Mitgliedern des Hauses (§ 14) „Prinzen“ und „Prinzessinen“ (§ 15). Trotzdem fehlt jedes Wort über Ebenbürtigkeit. Also ist anzunehmen, daß auch Herzog Alfred bezüglich der Ehevoraussetzungen alles beim alten, d. h. bei dem Rechte vor dem Erwerb der Landeshoheit belassen wissen will.

Dies ist um so mehr anzunehmen, als die Fideikommißurkunde über eine andere Ehevoraussetzung sich völlig ausschweigt, über die der Heiratsbewilligung durch das Haupt des Hauses. Sie spricht von einem „Chef des Hauses“ (§ 14), aber das Recht des Ehekonsenses legt sie ihm nicht bei. Das Abhängigmachen der fürstenrechtlichen Gültigkeit der Ehe von einer Heiratserlaubnis des Familienhauptes ist eine Einrichtung, die sich erst im 19. Jahrhundert beim Hochadel einbürgerte. Indem das neue Hausgesetz sie nicht aufnahm, bekundet es zugleich den Grundsatz, es für die Ehevoraussetzung überhaupt beim alten zu lassen.

Wir sind aber nicht nur auf Vermutung und Schlußfolgerung angewiesen. Das Hausgesetz von 1860 spricht auch selbst aus, daß für die Nachfolge und demgemäß auch für die Erfordernisse hierzu es beim alten Hausrecht nach wie vor verbleiben soll. Aus zwei Stellen geht dies hervor. In der Einleitung sagt Herzog Alfred, wie bereits einmal erwähnt: Durch die provisorische Verordnung vom 22. Oktober 1803 hat mein Großvater die von altersher in meiner Familie bestandene Sukzessionsordnung nach dem Rechte der Erstgeburt auch auf das Amt Dülmen übertragen. Und der die Nachfolge in das Fideikommiß verordnende § 4 beginnt mit den Worten: Dieses vorbestimmte Fideikommiß soll dem alten Herkommen in meinem Hause und der Verordnung meines Großvaters entsprechend eine Primogenitur, unter Ausschluß der weiblichen Deszendenz sein. Somit Anerkennung und Erneuerung einer von dem gemeinen Fürstenrecht inhaltlich abweichenden Rechtsordnung.

c) Der Wille, die alten Voraussetzungen für den Erwerb der Hauszugehörigkeit beizubehalten, stimmt dann auch noch zu folgendem. Dieses Fortgelten dessen, was bisher im Hause galt, wird von drei staatlichen Rechtsakten vorausgesetzt.

Im Jahre 1803 werden „die Reste des Amtes Dülmen“ dem „Herzog von Croy“ zugeteilt. Es wird damit also erklärt, diese Reste sollen im Hause Croy erblich sein: somit Reste eines Amtes, kein großer Besitz, keine Grafschaft, kein Fürstentum in einem herzoglichen Hause. Deshalb geht der Reichsdeputations-Hauptschluß davon aus, daß die Vererbung so geschieht, wie der Herzogstitel sich vererbt.

Zweitens wird das Haus Croy 1815 zu einem mittelbar gewordenen Reichsstand im Sinne der Bundesakte Art. 14 erklärt. Dieser kennt nach dem Titel drei Arten solcher Reichsstände: mittelbar gewordene Fürsten, Grafen und Herren. Weil es herzoglich war, wurde das Haus Croy dem Titel nach einem reichsständischen Fürstenhause gleichgestellt. Die Bundesakte erteilt die dort vorhandenen Privilegien dem Hause. Also geht sie davon aus, daß sie denjenigen zukommen, die nach Hausrecht zum Hause gehören, sein Haupt und seine Glieder sind. Dem folgte auch die Praxis. 1825 wird beschlossen, die Fürsten sollen das Prädikat Durchlaucht erhalten. Wer Fürst im Hause sei, wurde nach Hausrecht bestimmt.

Die preußische Verordnung vom 12. Oktober 1854 beruft zur Ersten Kammer mit erblicher Berechtigung die nach der deutschen Bundesakte zur Standschaft berechtigten Häupter der vormaligen deutschen reichsständischen Häuser in Preußen. Grundlage der Berufung und des Erbrechts hiezu bildet somit der standesherrliche Besitz in Preußen, aber berufen wird das Haupt des Hauses. Deshalb wird vorausgesetzt, daß für Nachfolge in die Standesherrschaft und in die Hauptstellung dieselben Grundsätze gelten. Mit der Hauptstellung ist beim Hause Croy der Herzogtitel verbunden. Er ist französischer Verleihung. Demgemäß ist vorausgesetzt, daß für den Erwerb der Standesherrschaft keine anderen Voraussetzungen gelten, als für den Erwerb des Haustitels. Beides soll nicht auseinanderfallen. Dies würde aber eintreten können, wenn für den Erwerb der Standesherrschaft Ebenbürtigkeit erforderlich wäre. Der Ebenbürtige könnte nicht Herrenhausmitglied werden, weil er nicht den Herzogstitel, und der Nichtebenbürtige nicht, weil er nicht die Standesherrschaft besitzt. Der Ebenbürtige erwürbe nur die Herrschaft, der andere lediglich den Titel.

3. Die bisherigen Beweise sind allgemeiner Natur. Sie betreffen die Sukzessionsordnung als ganzes, sind Ableitungen hieraus. Nun noch ein besonderer Beweis, d. h. ein Beweis unmittelbar aus dem Rechte der Ehevoraussetzungen dafür, daß im Hause Croy für die Ebenbürtigkeitsfrage Sonderfürstenrecht gilt.

Eine Vorschrift, aber auch nur eine über Ehevoraussetzung findet sich im Hausgesetze von 1860.

Die Vorschriften über die Erbfolgeordnung stehen in § 4. Hier heißt es zum Schluß nach dem Satze, daß der, an den beim Übergang an den Weibesstamm das Gut fällt, Name und Wappen der Familie Croy anzunehmen hat, in einem neuen Absatze: „Uneheliche Kinder sollen von der Sukzession in das Fideikommiß gänzlich ausgeschlossen sein und auch keinen Anspruch auf die Apanage haben.“ Die Vorschrift mag bedeuten, was sie will, also: auch wenn Ehelichwerden nachfolgt, oder: auch die unehelichen Kinder von Töchtern oder auch: wenn der oder die Uneheliche letzter Abkömmling des Hauses ist. Und die Vorschrift wird alles dies bedeuten. Wichtig ist, daß lediglich diese eine Regel über die Ehefrage sich findet. Warum allein dieser Satz? Die zutreffende Auslegung gibt der geschichtliche Zusammenhang. Lediglich diese Voraussetzung haben die Titeldiplome des Hauses gemacht. Der Titel: „Prince de Solre“ an Stelle von Comte de Solre beruht auf einem Diplome des Königs Karl II. von Spanien vom 4. November 1677. Er wird verliehen an alle Erben und Nachfolger, mâles et femelles, nés et à naître en leal mariage, somit an alle Söhne und Töchter aus gültiger Ehe. Und ebenso ist es bei den Lettres Patentes Ludwigs XVI., durch die 1788 der Titel „Duc de Croy“ geregelt wird. Hier heißt es am Schlusse, daß den Titel sollen gebrauchen dürfen: notre dit cousin, ensemble ses enfants et descendants en ligne directe nés et à naître en legitime mariage. Somit auch hier: Geburt aus gesetzlicher Ehe, das ist die einzige Voraussetzung für den Titelerwerb und damit für die Hausmitgliedschaft. Dieser Satz ist stillschweigend übernommen worden in das Nachfolgerecht des regierend und später hochadelig werdenden Zweiges und, als dieser Zweig dann der einzige war und das Haupt desselben 1860 ein Fideikommiß aus seinen deutschen Besitzungen errichtete, hat der Stifter ihn deshalb beibehalten.

Bei der Rentei Dülmen findet sich ein Akt Fach 7 Nr. 1 mit der Aufschrift: Herzog Alfred: Testaments- und Fideikommiß-Entwürfe. Hieraus geht hervor, daß die Stiftungsurkunde im wesentlichen das Werk des Herzogs Alfred selbst und seiner Dülmer Domänialverwaltung ist. Auf Blatt 28 begegnen wir einem vom Herzog eigenhändig geschriebenen Entwurf, der die Überschrift trägt: „Entwurf zu einer Fideikommiß-Stiftung in Form eines Testaments, meine Wünsche enthaltend, die ich in gesetzlicher Form einzukleiden bitte.“ Hier heißt es nach Aufzählung der Güter, die das Fideikommiß umfassen soll: „Dieses Majorat... soll nach meinem Tode auf meinen ältesten Sohn, Prinz Rudolf von Croy, übergehen, und nach ihm seiner männlichen Deszendenz nach Ordnung der Erstgeburt; sollte er keine männlichen Erben hinterlassen, dann soll es jenen meinen jüngeren Söhnen zufallen nach Ordnung der Erstgeburt, und sollten auch diese keine männliche legitime Erben hinterlassen, dann geht es auf jene meines zweiten Bruders über; und immer so fort nach der Regel der Erstgeburt; nur beim Erlöschen der männlichen Erben sollen die Töchter und dann zwar auch die älteste das Majorat erben.“ Der Entwurf ist ohne Datum. Er scheint 1848 niedergeschrieben zu sein. Jedenfalls geht aus ihm hervor: männliche Deszendenz ist ihm gleichbedeutend mit männlichen legitimen Erben. Im ganzen Akte wird kein Wort weiter darüber verloren.

Die geschichtliche Auslegung ist es, die somit auch hier den richtigen Weg weist. Auch die Ehepraxis des Hauses stimmt dazu. Die Agnaten des Hauses haben auch nach 1803 und 1815 vorwiegend Damen des französischen Adels geheiratet. Dem Hause Croy schien zur Erhaltung des Familienglanzes kein weiteres rechtliches Erfordernis notwendig. Unmöglich hätte sonst die von Prinz Alfred Emanuel 1875 zu London mit einer Bürgerlichen, der Kaufmannstochter Elisabeth Marie Parnell, geschlossene Ehe über ein Vierteljahrhundert unangefochten bleiben können. Anstandslos wurde die Frau des Prinzen als Prinzessin tituliert, auch vom Haupte des Hauses. Der Wandel der Auffassung 1903 in Einem Falle — der Chef des Hauses vertrat damals die gegenteilige Ansicht — hat kein das geltende Recht änderndes Herkommen begründet. Das Haus war ausländischer Herkunft und heiratete auch nach 1803 und 1815 vorwiegend ausländisch. Das Ausland kennt das Ebenbürtigkeitserfordernis nicht. Daher blieb das Haus bei diesem Grundsatz, auch als es hochadelig geworden war. Das Haus Croy ist ein außergewöhnliches deutsches hochadeliges Haus, nämlich ein aus dem Ausland stammendes. Demgemäß gilt in ihm auch außergewöhnliches, besonderes Privatfürstenrecht.

III. Ich fasse zusammen:

Das herzogliche Haus Croy ist hochadelig, aber Mitglied in ihm wird auch, wer aus einer unebenbürtigen Ehe abstammt.

Schriften der Wissenschaftlichen Gesellschaft in Straßburg:

Heft 1: Der Papyrus Libbey. Ein ägyptischer Heiratsvertrag. Von *W. Spiegelberg*. Mit drei Tafeln in Lichtdruck. 4°. IV, 12 S. 1907. ℳ 4.—

Heft 2: Arabische Beduinenerzählungen: Arabischer Text. Von *Enno Littmann*. 4°. VII, 58 S. 1908. ℳ 8.—

Heft 3: Arabische Beduinenerzählungen: Übersetzung. Von *Enno Littmann*. Mit 16 Abbildungen im Text. 4°. XI, 57 S. 1908. ℳ 6.—

Heft 4: Die griechischen Martyrien. Rede, gehalten bei der ersten Jahresversammlung der Wissenschaftlichen Gesellschaft in Straßburg am 6. Juli 1907. Von *Albert Ehrhard*.

Mit Anhang: 1. Jahresbericht der Wissenschaftlichen Gesellschaft in Straßburg, erstattet bei der ersten Jahresversammlung am 6. Juli 1907 von Adolf Michaelis. Mit dem Verzeichnis der Mitglieder der Gesellschaft. 4°. 30 und 8 S. 1907. ℳ 3.—

Heft 5: Studien zu Quintilians größeren Deklamationen. Von *R. Reitzenstein*. 4°. IV, 90 S. 1909. ℳ 9.—

Heft 6: Über die pseudoapostolischen Kirchenordnungen. Von *E. Schwartz*.

Mit Anhang: 2. Jahresbericht der Wissenschaftlichen Gesellschaft in Straßburg, erstattet am 4. Juli 1908 von Adolf Michaelis. 3. Jahresbericht der Wissenschaftlichen Gesellschaft in Straßburg, erstattet am 3. Juli 1909 von Theobald Ziegler. Mit dem Verzeichnis der Mitglieder der Gesellschaft. 4°. IV, 40 und 15 S. 1910. ℳ 4.—

Heft 7: Bußstufen und Katechumenatsklassen. Von *E. Schwartz*. Lex. 8°. IV, 61 S. 1911. ℳ 3.50

Heft 8: Griechische Urkunden des Ägyptischen Museums zu Kairo. Von *Friedrich Preisigke*. Lex. 8°. VIII, 58 S. 1911. ℳ 3.20

Heft 9: Venezianisch-Istrische Studien. Von *Walter Lenel*. Mit 3 Tafeln in Lichtdruck. Lex. 8°. XV, 197 S. 1911. ℳ 10.50

Heft 10: Zur nordarischen Sprache und Literatur. Vorbemerkungen und vier Aufsätze mit Glossar. Von *Ernst Leumann*. Lex. 8°. VIII 147 S. 1912. ℳ 9.60,

Heft 11: Die juristische Persönlichkeit der standesherrlichen Familie. Von *Hermann Rehm*. Lex. 8°. VI, 76 S. 1911. ℳ 3.—

Heft 12: Burzōes Einleitung zu dem Buche Kalīla waDimna. Von *Theodor Nöldeke*. Lex. 8°. V, 27 S. 1912. ℳ 1.50

Heft 13: Ein Erbstreit aus dem ptolemäischen Ägypten. Von *Otto Gradenwitz, Friedrich Preisigke, Wilhelm Spiegelberg*. Mit vier Tafeln in Lichtdruck. Lex. 8°. VII, 62 S. 1912. ℳ 6.—

Heft 14: Das tausendjährige Jubiläum der deutschen Selbständigkeit. Rede, gehalten in der Wissenschaftlichen Gesellschaft zu Straßburg, am 1. Juli 1911. Von *Harry Bresslau*.

Mit Anhang: 4. und 5. Jahresbericht der Wissenschaftlichen Gesellschaft in Straßburg, erstattet von Theobald Ziegler. Mit dem Verzeichnis der Mitglieder der Gesellschaft. Lex. 8°. III, 16 und 17 S. 1912. ℳ 1.20

Heft 15: Der Alexandersarkophag aus Sidon. Von *Franz Winter*. Format 57 × 50 cm. 18 Seiten Text und 18 Tafeln in Faksimile-Farben-Lichtdruck. 1912. In Mappe ℳ 120.—

Heft 16: Die standesherrliche Schiedsgerichtsbarkeit. Ihre Zulässigkeit und ihre Grenzen im heutigen Rechte. Denkschrift im Auftrage des Vereins der deutschen Standesherren verfaßt von *Hermann Rehm*. Lex. 8°. V, 57 S. 1912. ℳ 2.40

FSC
www.fsc.org
MIX
Papier | Fördert gute Waldnutzung
FSC® C083411

Kolibri 360 GmbH
Ferdinand-Jühlke-Straße 7
99095 Erfurt, Deutschland
produktsicherheit@kolibri360.de